Requiem for Battleship Yamato

REQUIEM FOR
Battleship Yamato

YOSHIDA MITSURU

Translation and Introduction by

RICHARD H. MINEAR

BLUEJACKET BOOKS

NAVAL INSTITUTE PRESS
ANNAPOLIS, MARYLAND

Originally published by the University of Washington Press
with the assistance of a grant from the Japan Foundation.
First Bluejacket Books printing, 1999

Library of Congress Cataloging-in-Publication Data

Yoshida, Mitsuru.
  [Senkan Yamato no saigo.   English]
  Requiem for Battleship Yamato / Yoshida Mitsuru ;
translation and introduction by Richard H. Minear.

     p.   cm.

   ISBN 1-55750-544-6

  1. Yamato (Battleship)   2. World War, 1939–1945—Naval
operations, Japanese.   3. World War, 1939–1945—Personal
narratives, Japanese.   4. Yoshida, Mitsuru.   I. Minear, Richard H.
II. Title.
D777.5.Y33Y6713   1999
940.54'5952—dc21   98-54794

To the memory of Takashima Eiko,
tutor at her home in Kyoto to generations of foreigners,
my principal tutor for three years; and
to the other native speakers who instructed me in Japanese,
whether in Japan or in America, most notably
Teruko Craig, Inoki Takenori, Itasaka Gen,
Matsuki Miyako, Miyo Okada, Schindō Eiichi,
and Takami Toshihiro.

ACKNOWLEDGMENTS

This is my first major translation project, and my debts are many and varied. The first debt is to those mentioned in the dedication, the native speakers who played so important a role in my formal language training. It is now twenty-five years since I began to study Japanese in the summer of 1960; I hope I have another twenty-five years to continue that study. Formal tutoring came to an end in 1971; but friends and colleagues have been most generous with their time and knowledge in continuing the process.

Libraries and librarians played their role. Frank Joseph Shulman, Director of the East Asia Collection of McKeldin Library at the University of Maryland, forwarded to me copies of the Gordon W. Prange Collection's file on *Requiem* and permitted me to quote from it. D. C. Allard of the Operational Archives Branch of the Naval Historical Center in Washington, D.C., Mitsuko Ichinose of the East Asian Collection at Yale University, and William T. Murphy of National Archives all responded promptly to inquiries.

As always, I have leaned on colleagues at the University of Massachusetts. Ching-mao Cheng and William Naff helped me with problems of translation. Hugh Bell showed endless patience with my queries about nautical terms and expressions. Tadanori Yamashita of Mount Holyoke College, a Five College colleague, spent long hours going over an initial draft.

Among many who read the manuscript in one or more of its incarnations and offered comments and encouragement, I can mention only the following: John J. Conway, John W. Dower, G. Barbara and the late Donald Einfurer, Peter Grilli, Mary Lewis, Joyce McDonough, my parents Paul and Gladys Minear, Mark Perry, Roger Pineau, Hajime Sakai, Robert N. Smith, Frederick W. Steinbeck, Henry I. Tragle, the late Robert G. Tucker, H. Leland Varley, the late R. G. Vliet.

Hiroaki Sato, initially a reader for University of Washington Press, was kind enough thereafter to give the entire manuscript a close reading. He also forwarded it to Charles Deroko and George Matteson for their comments. I am greatly in their debt.

Yoshida Yoshiko, widow of the author, showed a deep interest from the first. After several years' correspondence, we met for the first time in Tokyo in June 1983. Her warm support I acknowledge gratefully. Thanks to Mrs. Yoshida, I received assistance as well from Azuma Mafumi, Hara Katsuhiro, Nakai Haruo, and Tsukasa Tadayuki. Captain Baba Toshihaya (Maritime Self Defense Force), commanding officer of Air Station Atsugi, went through the entire manuscript with great care; the final translation is much sounder thanks to his efforts.

Etō Jun first brought this memoir to my attention. As the Translator's Introduction indicates, I do not see eye to eye with Etō; but I do thank him for his encouragement and assistance. Sodei Rinjirō took an early interest in this project and sent me useful material.

Most helpful of all was Yasuko Fukumi, librarian for East Asian Studies at the University of Massachusetts here in Amherst. She located materials for me in Amherst and in Tokyo; she went over many drafts with a dedicated and accurate eye, spending long hours with me discussing the text; she enlisted the help of family and friends in Japan—Fukumi Sachiko, Satō Tomoko, and especially Sayama Jirō and Sayama Kyōko—and Amherst in her determination that Yoshida's memoir receive the treatment it deserves; she assisted in my correspondence with people in Japan. I could not have asked for more support; she was always ready to help and always cheerful in helping. I hope this translation lives up to her hopes.

My agent Bonnie Crown was indefatigable in her pursuit of a press; she also commented helpfully on text and layout. At the University of Washington Press, Don Ellegood, Julidta Tarver, and Bruce Wilcox guided the manuscript through; Gretchen Swanzey made a very large number of most useful editorial suggestions; and Audrey Meyer was responsible for developing the book's format. I am indebted also to Nobuki Saburō and Stephen Shaw of Kodansha Ltd. for kind treatment and editorial suggestions.

Despite all this help, there are still errors in this translation; they are mine.

Japanese Names and Terms

Throughout I have rendered names in their Japanese order: family name first, given name second. Yoshida is the author's family name; Mitsuru, his given name. Similarly, I have referred to geographical places by their Japanese names: Ōsumi Strait, for example, rather than Van Diemen Strait.

TRANSLATOR'S INTRODUCTION

Requiem for Battleship Yamato is Yoshida Mitsuru's story of his own experience as a junior naval officer in April 1945, when *Yamato* set out on a last and desperate sortie. As with most great battle stories, its ultimate concern is less bombs and bullets than human nature, less death than life. It has long been a minor classic in Japan; this is the first full translation into any other language.

The Battle for Okinawa, April–June 1945

Situated 600 kilometers southwest of the island of Kyūshū, Okinawa was the last stop on the Allied drive to Japan—last, that is, except for the main islands themselves. American forces landed on Okinawa on 1 April 1945. The Japanese responded with counterattacks on land, with aerial suicide attacks by pilots flying from Kyūshū, and with the final task force sortie of the Imperial Japanese Navy. *Requiem for Battleship Yamato* tells the story of that sortie.

Well before the American assault on Okinawa, the Pacific War had swung decisively against Japan. True, Japan did not surrender until August; but the fact that fighting continued that long is attributable primarily to the war's own inertia and the tunnel vision of leaders on both sides. Events of June 1944, ten months earlier, foretold the end.

June 1944 witnessed the American assault on the southern Marianas—Saipan, Tinian, and Guam. Saipan and Tinian fell in June, Guam in July. Japan reacted to the American assault on the Marianas by amassing its remaining naval and air power to launch a counterattack. Before this battle the chief of the Japanese navy's general staff repeated the words spoken first by Admiral Tōgō before the battle of Tsūshima in 1905: "The fate of the Empire hangs on the outcome of this battle." The battle of Tsūshima had ended in a stunning Japanese victory; the fighting of June 1944 ended in a stunning Japanese defeat. The American forces damaged or destroyed five Japanese carriers, one battleship, three cruisers, and three tankers. More telling still, the Japanese lost over four hundred planes and pilots (the Americans soon dubbed the battle "the great Marianas turkey shoot"). In Tokyo the fall of Saipan precipitated the fall of the cabinet of Prime Minister Tōjō.

With the fall of the southern Marianas, Japan proper for the first time fell within range of land-based aircraft, the new superfortress B-29s. Once the existing runways had been repaired and lengthened, the enormous fleet of B-29s rained destruction on the four main islands of Japan. The first B-29 raid on Tokyo took place on 24 November 1944. B-29s from the Marianas carried out the firebombing of Tokyo on 9 March 1945. B-29s from Tinian carried the atomic bombs to Hiroshima and Nagasaki on 6 August and 9 August. But well before August, Japan's fate had been sealed, for by the end of March 1945 the American forces had retaken the Philippines, captured Iwojima, and placed the home islands under virtual blockade. With the advantage of hindsight, we can see that the Pacific War was over well before the battle for Okinawa began. But smaller views prevailed, and the war went on.

Planning for the Allied assault on Okinawa began in October 1944.[1] Operation Iceberg was "the most audacious and complex enterprise yet undertaken by the American amphibious forces."[2] Fleet Admiral Chester W. Nimitz had overall command of 1,500 ships and 250,000 men.

One hundred thousand men of the Imperial Japanese Army constituted the land defense of Okinawa. Ten ships formed the task force whose fate is described in this memoir: battleship *Yamato* (Rear Admiral Ariga Kōsaku, captain), light cruiser *Yahagi,* and eight destroyers. Vice Admiral Itō Seiichi was in direct command of the task force; his headquarters was in *Yamato. Yahagi* and the eight destroyers made up the Second Destroyer Squadron; it was commanded by Rear Admiral Komura Keizō, with headquarters in *Yahagi.* Ultimate control rested with Admiral Toyoda Soemu, commander in chief of the Combined Fleet, whose headquarters was near Tokyo.[3]

The Allies landed first on 26 March not on Okinawa

1. There are many treatments of the Okinawa campaign. Especially useful are Samuel Eliot Morison, *Victory in the Pacific, 1945,* vol. 14 of his *History of United States Naval Operations in World War II* (Boston: Little, Brown, 1960), pp. 79–282; and Roy E. Appleman et al., *Okinawa: The Last Battle,* one volume in the series United States Army in World War II: The War in the Pacific (Washington: Historical Division, Department of the Army, 1948).

2. British Combined Operations Observers Pacific Ocean Areas Report, 18 April 1945, quoted in Morison, *Victory,* p. 86.

3. For the Japanese side of the Okinawa campaign, see in English Paul S. Dull, *A Battle History of the Imperial Japanese Navy (1941–1945)* (Annapolis: Naval Institute Press, 1978); Masanori Ito with Roger Pineau, *The End of the Imperial Japanese Navy,* trans. Andrew Y. Kuroda and Roger Pineau (New York: W. W. Norton, 1962); and Saburo Hayashi with Alvin D. Coox, *Kōgun: The Japanese Army in the Pacific War* (Quantico: The Marine Corps Association, 1959).

itself but on the Kerama Island group 24 kilometers to the west. The initial landing on Okinawa came at 0830 hours on 1 April. The Japanese chose not to contest the landing, but fighting thereafter was fierce. The island was not declared secured until 21 June.

Between 6–7 April and 21–22 June the Japanese launched ten waves of suicide planes against the American fleet. Code name for the entire operation was *Kikusui* (the chrysanthemum crest of Kusunoki Masashige, loyalist hero and martyr of the fourteenth century). The navy's part of the operation, the sortie of 6–7 April involving battleship *Yamato* and nine escort ships, received the code name *Ten'-ichigo*. *Ten* means heaven; as Yoshida speculates in *Requiem,* it came from the phrase "a heaven-sent opportunity to reverse one's fortunes." *Ichigo* means number one (*ichi* is one, *go* is a counter). But *Kikusui* and *Ten'ichigo* were no match for Iceberg.

The disparity between the opposing forces is perhaps most evident in the casualty and damage figures. The American attackers lost just over 12,000 killed; the Japanese defenders, just over 110,000 (including 24,000 civilians). The attackers lost 763 planes; the defenders lost 7,830 planes. The attackers lost 36 ships sunk and 368 damaged; the defenders lost 16 ships sunk and 4 damaged—almost all Japan had to lose. As Paul S. Dull has written, "With the sinking of the great battleship *Yamato,* the once-formidable Imperial Japanese Navy had ceased to exist."[4]

4. Dull, *A Battle History,* p. 335.

Battleships and Battleship Yamato

In the years before 1941 most naval strategists considered battleships to be the epitome of naval power.[5] The pride of the British navy was its *King George V* class: 227 meters long and displacing 38,000 tons, these ships carried ten 356 mm. guns. The German navy boasted of *Bismarck* and *Tirpitz:* 251 meters long and displacing 46,000 tons, they each carried eight 380 mm. guns. During the war the United States Navy commissioned four battleships of the *Iowa* class: 270 meters long and displacing 49,000 tons, they carried nine 406 mm. guns.

Battleships *Yamato* and *Musashi* constituted Japan's attempt to outclass this competition.[6] Completed in 1940, these giants were 263 meters in length, longer than all but the *Iowa*-class battleships. They displaced 67,000 tons, outweighing even the Iowa class by 40 percent. Extraordinary steel armor accounted for that weight: armor 460 mm. thick protected the sides of the ship; armor 330 mm. thick protected the main tower; armor 500 mm. thick protected the conning tower. As additional protection, a flood-control system involved 1,150 watertight compart-

5. On battleships in general, see among many sources William E. McMahon, *Dreadnought Battleships and Battle Cruisers* (Washington: University Press of America, 1978).

6. For particulars of design, see Kitaro Matsumoto and Masataka Chihaya, "Design and Construction of the *Yamato* and *Musashi*," *U.S. Naval Institute Proceedings* 79, no. 10 (October 1953): 1102–13. See also Masataka Chihaya, "IJN Yamato and Musashi," in Anthony Preston, ed., *Warships in Profile*, vol. 3 (Garden City, NY: Doubleday, 1974), pp. 129–151; and Robert O. Dulin, Jr., "The *Yamato* Class— a design study," unpublished paper, U.S. Navy Department, Naval History Division, Operational Archives, 1961.

ments. *Yamato* and *Musashi* were thought to be unsinkable.

But most awesome of all was their firepower. Each ship had nine 460 mm. guns; that is, these guns fired shells *18 inches in diameter*. Each shell weighed 3,200 pounds (compact cars today weigh much less than that); and *Yamato*'s guns fired these enormous shells 44 kilometers—almost 30 statute miles!

To be sure, the battleship mentality that had held sway in the 1920s and 1930s was an early casualty of the Pacific War. The Japanese attack on Pearl Harbor turned the spotlight from battleships to aircraft carriers. Three days later, as if to underline the message, land-based Japanese airplanes sank the British battleship H.M.S. *Prince of Wales* and the battle cruiser *Repulse* off the coast of Malaya. Japan's two superbattleships would also succumb to concentrated air attack, *Musashi* off the Philippines in October 1944 and *Yamato* north of Okinawa in April 1945. Their fate confirmed the foresight of Admiral Yamamoto Isoroku, commander in chief of the Combined Fleet from 1940 until his death in 1943. In 1935, when the plans for *Yamato* and *Musashi* had been drawn up, Yamamoto was director of the navy's aeronautics department. An early proponent of naval air power, he had argued forcefully but to no avail against building the two super-battleships.

All these majestic battleships inspired awe in friend and foe. *Yamato*'s mystique was especially strong, in part because Yamato is the poetic name for Japan. Yamato had once been a place name used narrowly for the area around the early Japanese capital of Nara, but early on it became a broader designation for the nation as a whole. A Japanese emperor of the seventh century A.D. recorded his love for his land in this poem:

Countless are the mountains in Yamato,
But perfect is the heavenly hill of Kagu;
When I climb it and survey my realm,
Over the wide plain the smoke-wreaths rise and rise,
Over the wide lake the gulls are on the wing;
A beautiful land it is, the Land of Yamato![7]

Long before the twentieth century the term Yamato evoked among Japanese the emotions captured for Americans in such phrases as "America the beautiful" and "Columbia, the gem of the ocean."

Operation Ten'ichigo involved the last, hopeless sortie of the Imperial Japanese Navy and the death of Japan's only remaining super-battleship—high drama already. But battleship Yamato served also as metaphor: the end of battleship Yamato, the end of the Japanese empire. A requiem for one is in significant measure a requiem for the other, too.

Kamikaze—Special Attacks

Operation Ten'ichigo was a suicide mission. Few if any of the men expected to return alive. In Requiem Yoshida states that Yamato, like the kamikaze planes, had fuel enough for only a one-way trip. In fact, the task force had plenty of fuel, although that fact was a well-kept secret.[8] Still,

7. Emperor Jomei, "Climbing Kaguyama and looking upon the land," in Nippon Gakujutsu Shinkōkai, trans. and ed., The Manyōshū (New York: Columbia University Press, 1965), p. 3.

8. See, for example, Russell Spurr, A Glorious Way to Die: The Kamikaze Mission of the Battleship Yamato (New York: Newmarket, 1981), pp. 162–65.

fuel enough or no, Operation *Ten'ichigo* was a suicide mission roughly parallel to the missions in which Japanese pilots flew their planes—most were little more than bombs with wings—into American ships.

The first *kamikaze* operation took place in October 1944, well after the war had turned irrevocably against Japan. Indeed, the *kamikaze* were in large part a response to the prospect of imminent defeat. From the first, the Japanese used two terms to label these suicide attacks: *kamikaze* (or, less frequently, the same two characters read according to their Sino-Japanese pronunciation, *shimpū*) and *tokkō* (special attack).

The term *kamikaze* means divine wind. It appears in the *Kojiki* (Record of ancient things, compiled A.D. 712) as *kamukaze,* a term conventionally associated with Ise, site of the shrine of the Sun Goddess. Thus, a poem in the *Kojiki* attributed to Jimmu Tennō, legendary first emperor, begins with these lines[9]:

Kamukaze no	On the large rocks
Ise no umi no	Of the sea of Ise
Oishi ni . . .	Of the divine wind . . .

In the late thirteenth century Japanese scribes seized this classical reference to designate the ocean storms that twice protected Japan against the fleet of the invading Mongols. It was an easy step 650 years later to apply the same term to the suicide missions of 1944 and 1945.

In *Requiem* Yoshida speaks more often of *tokkō* (special

9. Romanization and translation are from Donald L. Philippi, trans. and ed., *Kojiki* (Tokyo: University of Tokyo Press, 1968), pp. 177, 429. See also Ivan Morris, *The Nobility of Failure* (New York: Holt, Rinehart and Winston, 1975), p. 445 n47.

attack). *Tokkō* is an abbreviation formed by combining *toku* and *kō,* the initial ideographs of the term "special attack unit" *(tokubetsu kōgekitai).* Near the end of *Requiem* Yoshida engages in a dialogue with himself about the meaning of his experience:

Did I really do my part? Did I look death in the face in the line of duty?

No. Didn't I submit to death quite willingly? Didn't I cloak myself in the proud name of special attack and find rapture in the hollow of death's hand?

The author of *Requiem* did not die in a *kamikaze* mission. Still, he took part in one, fully expecting to die. In many ways he was typical of the *kamikaze* pilots: young, well-educated, highly motivated, and entirely realistic about the probability—indeed certainty—of Japan's defeat. Few *kamikaze* had literary gifts of the order of Yoshida's, but many were his peers in motivation and in bravery.

Few phenomena have given rise to such misunderstanding as the *kamikaze* of the Pacific War. Here is Vice Admiral C. R. Brown, an eye-witness: "Among us who were there, in the Philippines and at Okinawa, I doubt if there is anyone who can depict with complete clarity our mixed emotions as we watched a man about to die in order that he might destroy us in the process. There was a hypnotic fascination to a sight so alien to our Western philosophy." A yet more compelling description comes from Tom Engelhardt, whose impressions were gained not in 1945 in the Pacific but in the 1960s watching late-night movies on television: "A speck on the horizon, faces tense, jokes fall away, it's the Kamikaze! Half man, half machine, an incomprehensible human torpedo bearing down from the peripheries of fanatical animate existence to pierce the armored defenses of the forces of Western democracy." [10]

Moreover, the Western world has often generalized from a misunderstanding of the *kamikaze* to Japan as a whole, and from Japan to a supposedly homogeneous Far East, making the *kamikaze* symptomatic of that supposed defect in the "Oriental mind": its failure to value life. General William C. Westmoreland put it most directly in the movie *Hearts and Minds:* "Well, the Oriental . . . doesn't put the same high price on life as does a Westerner. Life is plentiful, life is cheap in the Orient. And as the philosophy of the Orient expresses it, life is not important." This vicious stereotype is not Westmoreland's invention; it has been part of the mental baggage of generations of Europeans and Americans.

There is little material available in English which attempts to present the *kamikaze* in less pejorative fashion. The single most useful work is Roger Pineau's translation (1958) of a book by Inoguchi Rikihei and Nakajima Tadashi: *The Divine Wind: Japan's Kamikaze Force in World War II.* The book contains letters and papers left by *kamikaze* pilots; and the translation is a very able one. Unfortunately, it received little scholarly attention on publication.

More important—at least, more influential among scholars—is the chapter on *kamikaze* pilots in Ivan Morris' *The Nobility of Failure* (1975). Morris writes sympathetically of the pilots, drawing extensively on both the Inoguchi-Nakajima book and on Pineau's translation. He de-

10. Rikihei Inoguchi and Tadashi Nakajima, *The Divine Wind: Japan's Kamikaze Force in World War II,* trans. Roger Pineau (Annapolis: Naval Institute Press, 1958), p. 3; Tom Englehardt, "Ambush at Kamikaze Pass," *Bulletin of Concerned Asian Scholars* 3, no. 1 (1971): 68.

scribes the pilots as "quiet, serious, and above average in both culture and sensibility." Morris links them with earlier Japanese heroes, men like Yoshitsune in the twelfth century, Kusunoki Masashige in the fourteenth, and Saigō Takamori in the nineteenth. He describes them collectively as "individuals who waged their forlorn struggle against overwhelming odds . . . eager, outrageous, uncalculating men whose purity of purpose doomed them to a hard journey leading ultimately to disaster." Morris' *kamikaze* thus become another case study in Japanese national character, in a supposed "predilection for heroes who were unable to achieve their concrete objectives." [11]

The Nobility of Failure is an enormously stimulating book; but it may be unfair to the *kamikaze* and misleading to the reader to set the *kamikaze* into such a context. As Morris himself concedes, other traditions honor failed heroes. What tradition, in fact, does not? How else explain the fascination of Masada or the Alamo? Here is Bernard B. Fall's description of the last moments of the French Foreign Legion at Dienbienphu:

As the night fell over Dienbienphu that Friday evening—all the rest had fallen—the men could see the waves of enemy infantry surge toward them. Methodically they went about their business of destroying all the useless weapons and of caring for their wounded; and in the early dawn, led by their commander . . .

11. Morris, *Nobility of Failure*, pp. 306, xxii. Morris errs (p. 289) in stating that *shimpū*, not *kamikaze*, is the proper reading of the term as it applies to the suicide pilots of the Pacific War: "*Kamikaze* lacked the solemn, dignified ring of the Sino-Japanese equivalent and would have been quite unsuitable for the heroic exploits of 1944 and 1945." Evidence to the contrary includes popular songs of the time in which the only possible reading is *kamikaze*.

the Legionnaires fixed bayonets in the ghostly light of the parachute flares and—600 against 40,000—walked into death.[12]

Heroism is heroism; no nation or race has a monopoly on it or even an inside track. Yet it is all too easy to celebrate heroic action in a cause with which one identifies and denigrate heroic action on the part of an enemy. Many Americans might subscribe to an analysis linking the Alamo with American national character, Dienbienphu with French national character; in doing so, we identify *with* the heroes and swell with pride. Most of us do not identify in any way with the *kamikaze*. And when we seek to understand their deeds, we leap to "national character" explanations which become a putdown. Heroism becomes pathological, perverse, an innate fanaticism.[13] In reading this memoir the reader may well consider whether any resort to a putative Japanese national character is useful in explaining the author's reactions to his experience. No nation has a monopoly on heroism; nor, apparently, is any nation backward in the construction of myths sanctifying the sacrificial deaths of young men.

Yoshida Mitsuru

Yoshida Mitsuru was born in Tokyo in 1923 and died there in 1979. In 1943 he was an undergraduate student in law at Tokyo Imperial University, the training ground

12. Bernard B. Fall, *Street without Joy* (Harrisburg, Pa.: Stackpole, 1961), p. 285.

13. Cf. my review of Spurr, *A Glorious Way to Die*, in *The Progressive*, February 1981, pp. 57–58.

for the prewar elite, when he was called up into the Imperial Japanese Navy. One year later, as he writes at the opening of *Requiem,* he was "serving as ensign, assistant radar officer, in *Yamato.*" During most of *Yamato*'s final battle Yoshida was on the bridge, an ensign among admirals, staying there until the last possible moment and surviving only through a long series of improbable lucky breaks. Demobilized at the surrender, in December 1945 he entered the service of the Bank of Japan and spent his entire career there, becoming in the early 1970s one of the bank's executive officers. In 1948 Yoshida converted to Christianity and was baptized into the Catholic Church. In 1949 he married Nakai Yoshiko, a Protestant, and in 1957 Yoshida himself joined the United Church of Christ in Japan.[14]

Yoshida joined the Imperial Japanese Navy directly out of college. Indeed, he was called up in the midst of his undergraduate education, given a brief training course, and posted to *Yamato.* Some of *Yamato*'s junior officers shared his background, but others were graduates of the naval academy. It should not surprise us that the two career tracks made for differing outlooks, and Yoshida carefully identifies his fellow officers as being either the one or the other. In translating the Japanese term for those called up out of school and given a brief training course, I have translated by analogy and spoken of Officer Candidate School.

14. For biographical data on Yoshida, see Yoshida Mitsuru, *Sekininsha no ketsudan* (The decisiveness of those in positions of responsibility) (Yokohama: Kanagawa Keizai Kenkyūjo, 1979). This pamphlet, which consists largely of the text of a speech Yoshida delivered in April 1979, was published after his death; it includes a brief chronology and bibliography. See also the memorial notice in the Newsletter of the *Nihon heiwa gakkai* 56, no. 1 (April 20, 1981): 28. In English, see the essays of Etō Jun listed in notes 23–26.

Within a year of the sinking of *Yamato*—that is, well before he reached his twenty-third birthday—Yoshida completed, virtually overnight, the first draft of this memoir. Thereafter he made many revisions, major and minor, before its first publication in 1952. Subsequent revisions were minor. In 1978, one year before his death, Yoshida issued what he termed the definitive edition; that text is translated here. We have already noted one instance of factual error in *Requiem*. This is not a history but a memoir, Yoshida's account of his own experiences and reflections. It does not pretend to be the definitive historical account of the sinking.

But *Requiem* is "one of the great pieces of writing" to come out of the Pacific war.[15] It was written at white heat in mid-October 1945. Long after the fact, in an informal colloquium in 1977, Yoshida spoke of his sense of mission in writing *Requiem*:

That aspect of things in which Japan—the Japanese—excels and that aspect of things in which Japan is very, how shall I say it, very one-sided: both aspects were present in the extreme in the death of *Yamato*. On thinking back after the fact, that is, I had that feeling. In that sense, you see, the death of *Yamato* had elements of the symbolic.

And then coming in out of the blue as a student, as I did, getting a year's accelerated training, becoming an ordinary combat officer, and then, just as the battle started, standing watch on the bridge—the ship was so huge that had I not been on the bridge, I would have had only a very limited view of things. So

15. The judgment is widely held; the words are those of the writer Shimao Toshio, himself a veteran (indeed, a member of a special attack unit). Shimao Toshio and Yoshida Mitsuru, *Tokkō taiken to sengo* (The special attack experience and postwar life) (Tokyo: Chūō kōronsha, 1978), p. 140.

in that sense I had the real feeling, still and all, that something or other caused me to write that document.[16]

Also in 1977 Yoshida wrote of the war's effect on him:

I was an average O.C.S. officer, a run-of-the-mill military man. Among the countless young men sent into battle at the end of the Pacific war, I was entirely unremarkable. It is only that the experience I was confronted with was unique, nothing more. It was my lot to undergo a tragic experience which exemplified an age, a people.

My postwar life, too, it is only fair to say, has been representative of the generation that experienced the war. Except that the weight of that unique war experience held me and did not let go. Leading an ordinary life in the postwar era, one who survived when most of my comrades died, I could not exist without pursuing the meaning that heavy experience held for me, for the Japanese, for the postwar era.[17]

Both the modesty and the insight are typical.

Four of Yoshida's major writings concern themselves directly with *Yamato* and her crew: *Requiem,* an essay on the Japanese American Kunio Nakatani (in the essay Yoshida uses the fictitious name Ōta Kōichi), an essay on the archetypal naval academy graduate Lieutenant Usubuchi, and a book on Vice Admiral Itō Seiichi, commander in chief of Task Force II from headquarters in *Yamato.*

During the 1960s and 1970s Yoshida published essays on a number of other topics: his own lost generation, his time in the United States, moral responsibility. In these essays Yoshida stresses two points. First, war is hell. Second, it is not enough merely to hate war. In "The responsibility of the individual soldier or sailor," Yoshida reflects

16. Ibid., p. 56.
17. Ibid., p. 136.

on the Pacific War, discussing those ideas that came to him only after the war, when defeat brought about "the rebirth of the 'human being' inside me." He is haunted by

the realization of the real misery of war. Even if we consider only those nearly 10,000 officers and men who took part in special attack missions, each one of us had come to that point bringing with him twenty or thirty years of life; but in the end, in the crucible of nothingness we call battle, all vanished like foam. It cannot be dismissed as the result of the malfeasance of bad officers; officers and men, good people and bad people all, without distinction, were crushed in the violence of "war." If it were the case that all those who participated in battle were alike lovers of war, and that therefore a meaningless death was the only proper reward, we could conclude that the tragedy was a fairly shallow one. But such is not the case. War is all-out destructive force running rampant; it is heedless and absolutely indifferent to the countless human beings involved, who are tormented by all sorts of passions and regrets. It is not something that can be dealt with by grabbing an officer, say the captain of a ship, and charging him with unfeeling and bellicose acts. One can plumb the real depths of the tragedy of war only by digging down much deeper. Why did this man become a career officer? Why did he pursue this sort of death? If society had not demanded of him this role—if, say, he had been given a role to play in a peaceful world—what kind of person could he have become? [18]

In "The lost generation" Yoshida alludes to the remarkable media coverage of the Vietnam War as a welcome development, for it brings the experience of war, or the almost-experience of war, to everyone. Given that sit-

18. "Ippeishi no sekinin" (The responsibility of the individual soldier or sailor), in Yoshida Mitsuru, *Senchūha no shiseikan* (Views on life and death of the wartime generation) (Tokyo: Bungei shunju, 1980), pp. 153–54.

xxvi

uation, he writes, there is "probably no need to head for the battlefield in order to experience the wretchedness of war. . . . Still, even though from time to time one is shocked at the barbarity, the pointlessness of war, one can never be shocked enough." [19] For Yoshida, war is hell. Although he is honest about the exaltation he and others experienced in battle, he concludes *Requiem* with the reflection: "How despicable the slightest pride in having seen active combat."

Constant awareness that war is hell is not enough. To quote again from "The responsibility of the individual soldier or sailor": "If war could be prevented simply by hating war, then there would have been few chances for war to take the historical stage." But of course, as he has just noted, human history has seen war more often than peace. He continues: "Still, mustn't hatred of war form the first foundation for the prevention of war? Isn't the core of any peace movement formed of people who individually and unceasingly keep alive in their own hearts the fires of hatred of war? In the final analysis, however, hatred is 'negation,' and for 'negation' to become a real force it must be backed up by 'affirmation.' " This affirmation is the desire for peace: "We long for peace unconditionally, for its own sake. We hate war without specific reason, absolutely. There can be no war that is in any sense desirable. 'War as a means to peace' is itself a contradiction in terms."

Characteristically, Yoshida looks for the meaning of peace in details of one's daily life: "Respect for humanity. The relentless pursuit of truth. Mutual trust and cooperation. The desire for progress." To be sure, such a state-

19. "Sange no sedai" (The lost generation), in Yoshida Mitsuru, *Senkan Yamato* (Battleship *Yamato*) (Tokyo: Kadogawa shoten, 1968), pp. 189–90.

ment of goals in and of itself does not specify the means one is prepared to employ. But here and elsewhere Yoshida includes political action as part of the individual's moral responsibility. To be effective, opposition to war must appear early. If such action comes down merely to accepting (or refusing) conscription in wartime, he writes, then the real battle has already been lost. Which of those individuals facing conscription during the Pacific War, he asks, had lifted even a finger against earlier governmental decisions? [20]

Yoshida calls for active involvement in politics, active working for peace and against war. But he seems less than sure that his voice will be heard. He concludes "The lost generation" with these words:

Has Japan, through defeat, graduated from war? To be sure, defeat gave the Japanese people a valuable experience, and the Peace Constitution was born; but have we truly escaped from the menace of war? Isn't it purely and simply a matter of luck that for these twenty years Japan has not been involved in war? Is that . . . any guarantee that there is no possibility war will erupt in our vicinity? Isn't it true that even in this postwar period of peace such eruptions have taken place in a great many countries?

Suppose that, unfortunately, war threatened in our vicinity. Would we be ready to stand up to it? On what points and how far have we progressed in comparison with the example of the wartime generation of those years, which was swept along so powerlessly and with no resistance and took the road of cooperation with the war? Can we say that we have made any preparations for firm "resistance to war" beyond the prudence of merely keeping our distance and not getting injured ourselves? [21]

20. "Ippeishi no sekinin," pp. 163–64.
21. "Sange no sedai," pp. 195–96.

Only one of Yoshida's writings, an essay on "The 'Space Cruiser *Yamato*' Generation," has appeared in English translation, in *Japan Echo* (6, no. 1 [1979]:80–87). That essay reminds us that for many Japanese today *Yamato* is first and foremost the name of the spaceship in an animated cartoon. To be sure, that spaceship is modeled on Yoshida's *Yamato;* but one can only speculate on the number of the cartoon's fans who know much at all about the real *Yamato*.

Occupation Censorship and *Requiem*

Yoshida arranged for the first version of *Requiem* to be published in the November 1946 issue of the journal *Sō-gen*. However, Japan in 1946 was under American Occupation, and prepublication censorship was one facet of Occupation activities. The initial censor reacted sympathetically to parts of the text, stating that "the young author reports, it seems, anything and everything as he saw and as he heard with his own eyes and with his own ears. There is very little exaggeration, if any, but the effect is so penetrating and touching."

But the censor considered the work as a whole objectionable. He wrote: "Here is an instance of the Japanese militaristic spirit . . . viewed from inside. The simple attitude of the author and the vivid style of *{Requiem}* as well as the extremely impressive contents themselves cannot fail to arouse in the mind of the readers something like deep regret for the lost great battleship, and who can be sure that the warlike portion of the Japanese do not yearn after another war in which they may give another *Yamato* a better chance?" Permission to publish was denied.

Yoshida tried repeatedly to alter the verdict of the censors. In 1948 the son of the new prime minister of Japan attempted to intervene with the authorities, but to no avail. In 1949 Yoshida rewrote *Requiem* in nonliterary Japanese and published it in a pulp magazine (*Salon,* June 1949); he also arranged for publication in book form. Summoned to appear before the censors on 5 July 1949, Yoshida and his publisher were given a severe dressing-down:

Yoshida was reprimanded for making suppressed material available to a publisher after repeated Civil Censorship Detachment reminders that the material had been suppressed and was very objectionable. . . . Yoshida was told that . . . CCD views very unfavorably the fact that, in spite of reminders that the action would not be changed, the material had been given to a publisher for printing. . . . [The publisher] was shown the portion[s] of the book *Battleship Yamato* which were considered objectionable . . . and advised to make heavy editorial cuts in the whole book before printing. He was told that this office under no circumstances [would] countenance printing of the suppressed . . . material. He was further advised to keep this office informed as to his intentions concerning the book.

This memorandum includes the following sad sentence: "Yoshida said that he now fully understood the position of this office and would make no further attempts to publish this material." [22] Only in 1952, after the writ of the Occupation had run out, did the full text of *Requiem* reach the

22. File on Yoshida Mitsuru's "The Last of the Battleship Yamato," Gordon W. Prange Collection of Publications and Unpublished Materials from the Allied Occupation of Japan, East Asia Collection, McKeldin Library, University of Maryland.

public. And only in 1981—thirty-five years after its composition and two years after the death of the author—did the original version of 1946 reach the public.[23]

The version that first drew the censor's ire is roughly one-fifth the length of the definitive text translated here. Many sentences from the former appear unchanged in the latter, but there are additions as well as alterations. For example, the final line of the original reads as follows: "The keenness of their fighting spirit and the high level of their skill made it an end of which one need feel no shame." That sentence does not appear in the definitive text.

In a recent essay, critic Etō Jun analyzes the differences between the censored original and the work as it was published in 1952. Although he had earlier referred to *Requiem* as "one of the best literary works . . . produced in postwar Japan,"[24] it is now his contention that the 1952 version is significantly altered both in content and in tone. Etō suggests that the censored original expresses Yoshida's true thoughts and constitutes greater literature, and that in the process of fighting the censors Yoshida "surrendered for the first time." Yoshida's earlier solidarity with his dead comrades and his honest antagonism to the American enemy gave way, contends Etō, to the more philosophical and dispassionate version translated here. Etō's critique is complicated by the context of his remarks: a broad attack on

23. Etō Jun, *"Senkan Yamato no saigo shoshutsu no mondai"* (The first appearance in print of *Requiem for Battleship Yamato*), *Bungakkai*, vol. 35, no. 9 (September 1981).

24. Etō Jun, "The Severed Tie with the Past: Literature and Occupation Censorship—The Case of Yoshida Mitsuru and the *Last of the Battleship Yamato*," typescript of lecture presented at the Wilson Center (Washington, D.C., 13 November 1979), p. 1.

the American Occupation and on the peace constitution.[25]

I hold no brief for censorship, and I find the reasons the censors offered for forbidding publication of *Requiem* unconvincing at best. But I do think Etō has overstated his case. Etō argues that Occupation censorship visited on Yoshida "a kind of spiritual death" in that it deprived him "of the image of the dead."[26] Censorship clearly hurt Yoshida, but how badly? Yoshida did not face death or exile for his writing. He had the praise of important literary figures who read the work in manuscript. He had friends in high places. And he surely knew that *Requiem* would be published in the near future. (In March 1947 MacArthur called for an early end to the Occupation; in May 1950 John Foster Dulles was assigned the task of negotiating a treaty.)

Form and Style

In form, *Requiem* is a diary or log: a series of brief entries. Almost all are from the point of view of the author; almost all are in the present tense. In reality, however, it is neither diary nor log but wholly a creation after the fact. Yoshida escaped the sinking *Yamato* with only his

25. Etō, *Senkan Yamato no saigo* shoshutsu no mondai," p. 155; Etō Jun, "The 1946 Constitution: Its Constraints," typescript of paper presented at the Wilson Center, 24 March 1980, expanded in a later Japanese version: "Senkyūhyakuyonjūrokunen kempō—sono hōsoku" (The 1946 constitution: its constraints), in *Shokun* 12, no. 8 (August 1980): 20–65, and 12, no. 9 (September 1980): 90–99.

26. Etō Jun, "The American Occupation and Postwar Japanese Literature: The Impact of Censorship upon a Japanese Mind," typescript, no date, no place, p. 16.

skin: no log, no notes, nothing. (Passages in the past tense represent not what Yoshida remembers thinking or feeling at the time, but reflections either at the time of his safe return or at the time of writing, several months later.)

Yoshida's style is distinctive. Its impact derives from three interrelated factors. First, it is terse, tight, spare. Many sentences are abbreviated, lacking verbs or even subjects: "2345 hours" is one. Paragraphs do not normally run more than three or four lines, and many consist of mere handfuls of words: "List: 35 degrees." This aspect of Yoshida's style can be reproduced in translation, although the elliptical nature of the original sometimes necessitates more extended handling in English.

Second, Yoshida writes in *bungotai*, a literary language still in use before 1945 primarily for certain distinct purposes: government documents, military documents, some forms of poetry. In the "Afterword" to the 1952 edition of *Requiem,* Yoshida explained that the language was not really a conscious choice on his part: ". . . it is not the case that I had a particular preference for *bungotai.* Nor did I specifically intend to use it. When I set down the first line, the line emerged, of itself, already *bungotai.* Why should that have been the case? If pressed, I would offer two reasons. The first is that the gravity and the emotion of the life-and-death experience are difficult to express in everyday language. The second is that when you have entered the thick of battle and attempt to portray it, the rhythm of 'combat' probably demands the tone that is characteristic of this style."[27] Yoshida's *bungotai* is at once terse and elegant, clipped and classic. Both the military censor and Etō Jun describe *Requiem* as a prose-poem.

27. *Senkan Yamato no Saigo* (Tokyo: Hokuyō sensho, 1978), pp. 169–70.

Third, Yoshida uses the *katakana* syllabary. Japanese has two parallel systems of transcription for the sounds not represented by Chinese characters. One system, *hiragana,* is used today almost universally: in letters, novels, newspapers, textbooks. The other, *katakana,* is used today primarily in telegrams and in transcribing words of foreign origin; before 1945 it was used more broadly, official government reports being one such use. Yoshida uses *katakana* throughout, thus emphasizing the sense of immediacy, of reading a military dispatch. (There are only two exceptions: the two letters from the mother of the *nisei* assistant communications officer.) No existing typeface could impart similar impact to an English text, unless, perhaps, the entire text were to be printed on Western Union tape. (The Kadokawa edition of 1968 uses *hiragana.* Many of its details also differ from the definitive text—the Hokuyōsha edition of 1978 translated here.)

A literal translation of the title of the definitive edition of Yoshida's memoir is *The End of Battleship Yamato (Senkan Yamato no Saigo).* But "end" is too awkward and superficial a rendering of the Japanese *saigo,* which is used primarily of the death of individuals and conveys a sense of tragedy, an awareness of impermanence. "Last moments" would be closer.

I have chosen "Requiem" because the work *is* a requiem. Indeed, Yoshida uses that title—*Requiem for Battleship Yamato (Chinkon senkan Yamato)*—for an edition of 1974 which includes not only the present work but also the two long essays on his fellow officers. (In other words, this translation of *Senkan Yamato* takes as its title the title Yoshida gives to another publication of which the present text makes up a major part but not the whole.) Moreover, consider the comment of Etō Jun, who calls the work "essentially a requiem for the dead, like a Noh play in which the ill-fated Heike heroes are fondly evoked from the land of oblivion and reproduce the battle scene in which they took so valiant a part."[28] As in Etō's statement, the term "requiem" should not exclude the resonances between Yoshida's epic and the specifically Japanese literary usages of the term *saigo*.

For naval terminology in English I have followed primarily Samuel Eliot Morison, most notably in speaking of "*Yamato*," not "the *Yamato*." Throughout, like Yoshida, I have used the metric system. In two passages Yoshida speaks of miles. In one of these (the final lines of the book), the unit is the nautical mile. In the other, a reference to "some tens of miles," it is not clear which unit Yoshida intends.

A Note on Sources

There is no biography of Yoshida Mitsuru. A year after his death, friends published privately a lengthy book of reminiscences about him: *Tsuioku: Yoshida Mitsuru* (Reminiscences of Yoshida Mitsuru; Tokyo, 1980). Also published posthumously, appended to the text of Yoshida's last speech, were a brief chronology of his life and a basic bibliography (see p. xxiii, n. 14, above).

Requiem for Battleship Yamato has appeared in numerous editions since 1952; as noted above, some differ in form and detail from the definitive text translated here. Yoshida also published a biography of Admiral Itō Seiichi: *Teitoku Itō Seiichi no shōgai* (Tokyo: Bungei shunju, 1977). His book

28. Yoshida Mitsuru, *Chinkon senkan Yamato* (Tokyo: Kōdansha, 1974); Etō, "The Severed Tie," p. 6.

of essays, *Senchūha no shi ikan* (Views of life and death of the wartime generation), first published by Bungei shunju in 1980, has recently been issued by the same publisher in paperback. A second book of essays, *Heiwa e no junrei* (A pilgrimage to peace), appeared in 1982 (Tokyo: Shinkyō shuppan).

This is the first complete translation of *Requiem* into any language. A partial translation into English appeared in 1952: Mitsuru Yoshida, "The End of *Yamato*," trans. Masaru Chikuami, ed. Roger Pineau, *United States Naval Institute Proceedings* 78, no. 2 (February 1952): 116–29. This partial version was condensed still further and published as "My Last Watch on the *Yamato*," *Reader's Digest,* September 1952, pp. 57–61.

Readers interested in pursuing the story of *Yamato* should turn first to the sources cited in the notes of this Introduction. Two other books dealing with *Yamato* merit mention. Hara Tameichi was captain of light cruiser *Yahagi* during the final sortie; he has written about the battle in the last section of Tameichi Hara with Fred Saito and Roger Pineau, *Japanese Destroyer Captain* (New York: Ballantine, 1961). A recent book includes an account of the battle based heavily on Yoshida's memoir: Dennis Warner and Peggy Warner with Sadao Seno, *The Sacred Warriors: Japan's Suicide Legions* (New York: Van Nostrand Reinhold, 1982).

Several readers of this translation have suggested that the closest counterpart to *Requiem* in recent times is Antoine de Saint-Exupéry's *Flight to Arras,* trans. Lewis Galantière (New York: Reynal & Hitchcock, 1942). Although not about a sea battle, *Flight to Arras* combines action and reflection in the manner of *Requiem.*

Ensign Yoshida Mitsuru, December 1944. In this month
Yoshida was graduated from OCS, received the rank of ensign, and was posted to *Yamato*. His twenty-second birthday is a month away; the sortie, four months away. *Yoshida
Yoshiko*

Yamato being fitted out, September 1941
Defense Audiovisual Agency

Yamato during trial runs, 1941
National Archives

Officers of *Yamato*'s first wardroom. Lieutenant Usubuchi
is at center of front row; Ensign Yoshida is fourth from left
in third row.   *Hara Katsuhiro*

Rear Admiral Ariga Kōsaku, captain of *Yamato*
Hara Katsuhiro

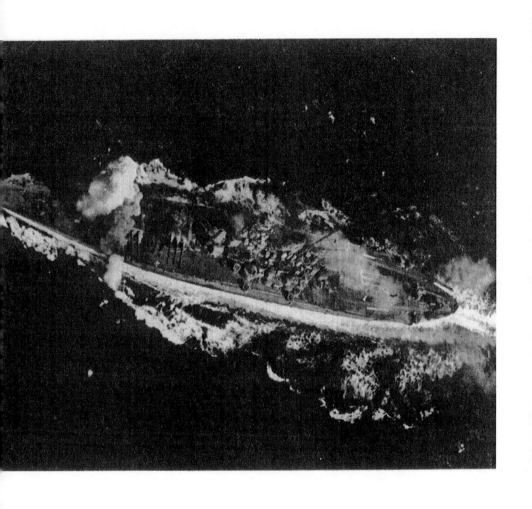

Yamato under attack in Philippine waters,
24 October 1944 *National Archives*

Yamato down in the bow and slowed, 7 April 1945
National Archives

Yahagi dead in the water   *National Archives*

Yamato under attack   *National Archives*

Yamato explodes   *National Archives*

The New

"All the News That's Fit to Print"

NEWS INDEX, PAGE 37, THIS SECTION

Copyright, 1945, by Th

VOL. XCIV. No. 31,851.

Entered as Second-Class Matter, Postoffice, New York, N. Y.

NEW YORK, S

U. S. FLIERS SINK JAP
BRITISH NEAR BREM
PATTON SEIZES NAZI

FOUR STABILIZERS ASK FIRM CONTROL BEYOND END OF WAR

Policy 'With Boldness' Is Vital to Prevent Any Runaway Inflation, They Assert

SAY 'LINE IS HELD' TO DATE

Davis, Bowles, Jones, Taylor Summarize Their Work in Report to Roosevelt

The report on price and wage control is on Page 34.

Special to THE NEW YORK TIMES.

WASHINGTON, April 7—A call for continuance of price and wage controls during the transitional period after the war to provide stabilization and guard against inflation was made to President Roosevelt today by the four officials who exercise primary responsibility in those fields. Their report told the Chief Executive that, to date, "essential stabilization has

309,258 Germans Seized in 2 Weeks

By The Associated Press.

PARIS, April 7—In one of the most dramatic fortnights of the war—since the Allies carried their offensive across the Rhine —the Germans have lost more than 309,258 troops in prisoners alone and roughly 18,000 square miles of territory east of that river.

The number of Germans captured since the Rhine crossing already exceeds the 250,000 captured in the three-week March mop-up west of the Rhine, which Gen. Dwight D. Eisenhower declared "one of the greatest victories of this or any other war."

The figure of 309,258 does not include the thousands catch of Army Group B pinned in the Ruhr or the other thousands of Army Group H caught in the western Netherlands.

PRESIDENT PRAISES RECONVERSION PLAN

Letter Hails Gardner for Idea of OWM Board to Stress Peacetime Abundance

VIENNA ARC WIDENS

Capital Is Three-fourths Ringed—Russians at Danube to North

ESCAPE GAP SHRINKS

Munich - Linz Trunkline Slashed—Red Army 12 Miles From Teschen

By The Associated Press.

LONDON, Sunday, April 8— Red Army tank columns, in a fourteen-mile sweep around western Vienna, three-fourths encircled the Austrian capital yesterday, leaving to the enemy garrison a twenty-four-and-a-half-mile escape gap, as other shock troops gained in a frontal assault through the city's streets.

By reaching the Danube River northwest of the city, Russian troops sliced across six of Vienna's escape routes and left the imperiled capital with only seven of an original twenty-two major rail-

ALLIES RACE A

British 13 Miles Bremen While Heads for Bruns

1ST CROSSES

Third Smashes German Attack— Gains 36 Mil

By DREW MIDDLE

By Wireless to THE NEW YORK

PARIS, April 7—Amer British armored forces from their bridgeheads e across the Weser River today an across the province of while on the left flank o vance the British Seventh Division struck northwa sitions that field reports only thirteen miles from early this afternoon.

Battered by the sledge blows of the armored colu harried by clouds of fight ers, Germany is falling

New York Times, April 1945

rk Times.

Company.

PRIL 8, 1945.

Including Magazine
and Book Sections.

LATE CITY EDITION
Fair and warmer today. Partly
cloudy, continued mild tomorrow.
Temperatures Yesterday—Max., 57 ; Min., 41
Sunrise today, 6:29 A. M.; Sunset, 7:28 P. M.

Section
1

TEN CENTS
New York City and Suburban Areas (15c Elsewhere)

'S BIGGEST WARSHIP;
HANOVER FLANKED;
ARD OF GOLD AND ART

JAPANESE FLEET REMNANTS BATTERED ANEW

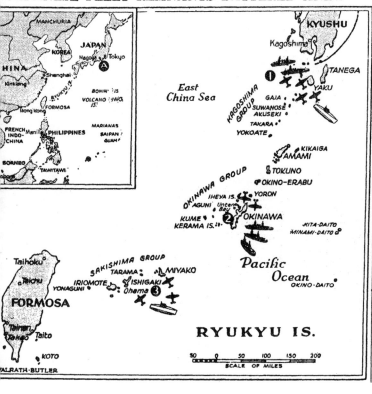

VICTORY IN PACIFIC

Carrier Planes Sink the Battleship Yamato and 5 Other Warships

BATTLE OFF KYUSHU

Foe Loses 417 Planes, Bulk of Them in Blow at Fleet Off Okinawa

By BRUCE RAE
By Wireless to THE NEW YORK TIMES.

GUAM, Sunday, April 8—The United States Fifth Fleet, after shattering an all-out Japanese aerial attack off Okinawa, on Friday (East Longitude time) launched a counter-offensive in the sky Saturday and delivered a smashing blow to the remnants of the Imperial Navy—sinking six warships, including the most powerful remaining unit, the battleship Yamato. The sinkings were in the East China Sea about fifty miles southwest of Kyushu, southernmost island of the Japanese home-

Seconds after the explosion   *Defense Audiovisual Agency*

Requiem for Battleship Yamato

At Anchor

Since the end of 1944, I have been serving as ensign, assistant radar officer, in *Yamato*.

March 1945. *Yamato* lies moored to Buoy 26 in Kure naval port. A large buoy, it is at the outer limit of the harbor.

In preparation for the coming mission, we are scheduled to make a hurried trip into dock for repairs to various parts of the ship and for the installation of recoilless guns, additional radar, and the like.

29 March, early morning: over the ship's P.A.— "Preparations for getting underway commence at 0815 hours; getting underway is scheduled for 1500 hours."

There has never been so sudden a sailing.

Is this it?

From the communications people, reports that wireless and signal traffic is heavy.

This is it—the sortie we've been waiting for. Being anchored "in preparation for entering the dock" was in fact a cover for our imminent departure.

Ten days ago seventy carrier-based American planes attacked our task force. That must have been a preemptive strike, with foreknowledge of our sortie.

How we have awaited this moment!

Ours is the signal honor of being the nation's bulwark. One day we must prove ourselves worthy.

3

As front-line officers and men, we have received more than our share of food and clothing. One day we must repay that treatment.

This sortie is our chance.

It also puts an end to intensive round-the-clock training and frees us from accumulated overwork and lack of sleep.

It is barely six days since the beginning of the bombardment of the Ryūkyūs by the American task force. The American landing on the Kerama Islands took place three days ago.

Our operation will probably take place in that general area.

Rumors sweep the vessel.

That we will pass through the Straits of Shimonoseki, be serviced and resupplied at Sasebo and refueled at Pusan, then head south.

Or that we will steam boldly straight south out of Bungo Channel.

Where will the operation take place? Which ships will accompany *Yamato?* How will the task force be organized?

Let's push forward and seek the decisive battle! Let's fight it out with the American task force!

Drowning out these whispers, the ship's penetrating P.A. transmits order after order.

"All divisions, bring flammable materials topside."

"All hands, secure all gear. Stow all personal gear below."

"Stand to preliminary readiness." (This means seal all passageway doors and the iron doors and hatches of all compartments for protection against fire and flooding.)

"Last boat for shore leaves at 0830 hours."

"All division officers, inspect for preliminary readiness immediately."

Orders and commands fly in all directions. How quickly the minutes pass!

Ordered to take charge of the last boat to shore, I take Launch One and head for Pier 1.

Thin clouds cover the sky; the surface of the water appears smoky; the streets of the port, seemingly asleep, are no different from usual.

The sea, undulating gently in its morning calm. The launch, moving straight ahead at full speed.

Arriving at the pier, I issue the necessary orders and make triple-sure no sailors are still on shore. To miss the sailing on the occasion of a mission is punishable by death before a firing squad.

But of course all sailors are already on board; there are no stragglers.

The thought occurs to me: will this be the last time I set foot on the soil of my native land?

At full speed we retrace our course to *Yamato*. A gentle breeze gladdens us.

Yamato's gigantic body of 73,000 tons, hull painted a uniform silver-white, displays on her sturdy prow the imperial chrysanthemum crest; titanic, immovable, *Yamato* dominates the scene.

Blinker flashes from *Yahagi* (new cruiser), moored near *Yamato:* "Preparations for getting under way completed . . ." On-off, on-off, briskly.

Back to *Yamato*. No need to stow my gear; I've done that long since. I turn immediately to preparations for getting under way.

Leaving Kure Harbor

1500 hours: *Yamato* leaves port. Serenely, the ship gets under way. It is the only ship in the harbor leaving port.

A quiet and composed sailing.

From sister ships at anchor, a million eyes alight with silent cheers focus on us.

They are counting on me: every last sailor filled with pride, we line up on deck.

To think that this was the final sailing, that this giant ship, now departing, would never return.

Passing quickly through Hiroshima Bay, we enter the channel.

I check that all radar instruments are in good working order and report to the division officer.

Taking advantage as usual of the changing conditions when the ship is under way, we begin antiair and antiship drill.

The ship's P.A.: "Scheduled to enter port at 1700 hours. All hands, muster at quarters when anchored."

Mustering at quarters? Orders for the sortie will be announced.

For practice we repeatedly turn and circle, but our course made good is for Suō Gulf.

The captain discusses tactics with staff (the staff officers of the task force).

On the chart stand, a thick document with red covers. In large letters on its spine: "Operation *Ten'ichigo.*"

Ten [heaven] probably comes from the phrase "a heaven-sent opportunity to reverse one's fortunes."

In the face of the all-out storming of Okinawa by the

6

American forces, won't heaven grant us divine resources to reverse the fortunes of this war?

The charts, several deep, are all detailed maps of the Okinawa area.

Set (in reduced scale) to the forty-kilometer range of *Yamato*'s main batteries, compasses describe an arc on the chart; its center is the point at which the American forces are expected to land. It must be the course proposed for this ship as she bombards the American forces on shore.

The fingernails of the staff officer wielding the compass turn white, so tight is his grip.

In suppressed voices the give-and-take continues. The makeup of the task force, the compass course, air cover, the time of sailing, and so on—a mountain of tough problems.

Waiting

Dusk: we drop anchor off Mitajiri. Having taken the shortcut directly through the narrows, a few destroyers have already preceded us into the harbor.

We left port separately in order to maintain secrecy and are now anchored temporarily in the roads here; contact with land still cut off, we await final orders for the sortie.

In the meantime, we seek in several days of rest to gain the strength to reverse the nation's fortunes, to hone our fighting spirit to the limits of selflessness.

We muster at quarters. All hands line up on deck in fatigues.

In the night, dark under blackout, the breathing of 3,000 men grows still.

The captain states the aim of the *Ten'ichigo* plan—to counter the American landing on Okinawa—and the mission of this vessel—to be the mainstay of the task force making the sortie; he voices his earnest hope that the men will all rise to the occasion and live up to the expectations of the entire navy.

The executive officer: "The time has come. *Kamikaze Yamato,* be truly a divine wind!"

Still without the order to sail, we spend the days idly at anchor, waiting.

1 April. The American landing on Okinawa. In the evening of the same day, they capture part of an airfield.

2 April. A report that the American task force is approaching, with strong probability of attack tomorrow. Does it hope to thwart us even before we get started?

I sleep in fatigues. Though my heart is impatient, I sleep soundly.

3 April, early morning: a report that the American force is attacking. We take our stations, leave the roads quickly, and spread out in Alert Formation I.

In Formation I the ships proceed fanned out, separated from one another by 1,500 meters, individual stations determined by the needs of scouting and defense; in this posture the front line is for protection against aircraft, the second, for protection against surface attack.

We wait, keeping up steam to be ready to respond to sudden attack.

From a cold start to the turning of the screws takes at least two hours of warming up.

We drift with the currents.

Our sortie should take place after the American task force has withdrawn. It won't do to rush things.

Forenoon: a single B-29 passes directly overhead and, from a high altitude, takes a blind shot at us. One middle-sized bomb. We are undamaged.

Still, might not the plane have performed photo reconnaissance? Has it already become impossible to conceal the movements of the task force?

Afternoon: radio reports come in at frequent intervals. Many sections of the main islands are under fierce aerial attack.

"Patience, patience," I urge myself over and over. Should our mission succeed, we will be able to reduce the destruction on the home front, if only by a little.

In the sky over the task force, a small formation of planes. They fly past as if to cut us off.

Each ship fires her guns, and one plane is knocked out of the sky; on the instant, the rest all urgently execute dives to display friendly insignia. We had mistaken Shidens from the Matsuyama squadron for Grummans.

In response to the strong protest of the commanding officer of the squadron, we reply by telegraph in the name of the task force commander: "Once the task force is in alert formation, it is a matter of course to shoot down all planes, friend or foe, that intrude unannounced onto the task force's course."

Having waited for the sun to set, we anchor temporarily once again in the roads where we have anchored the last several nights.

In this time of emergency, some fifty cadets, graduated a few days ago from the naval academy, come on board, brought alongside by *Daihatsu* (wooden launch).

9

Perhaps because of the honor of boarding *Yamato*, their ruddy cheeks glow even in the dusk. They divide into several groups and immediately set about touring the ship.

A fresh new spirit fills the air. How long before they develop into a true fighting force?

The radio intelligence unit attached to the communications division intercepts an urgent exchange of transmissions between American planes, translates it immediately, and reports to us on the bridge:

"After aerial bombardment of various targets throughout the day tomorrow, the American task force will withdraw to the east."

Will we put to sea in the wake of their withdrawal?

The sortie approaches. Night rations are delicious.

Ensign Nakatani, assistant communications officer, lies in his hammock, sobbing into his pillow. I pat him on the shoulder, and he produces a single sheet of writing paper.

He is a *nisei* from California. While attending Keiō University, he was drafted out of college; his two younger brothers are soldiers in the U.S. army, serving at present on the European front. He is a simple and good-natured young man, diligent in his work; he alone can pick up American emergency transmissions.

Nevertheless, because he is a *nisei,* the young active-duty officers look askance at him and have vilified him more than once in the presence of the whole group. At such times, as I am making my duty rounds late at night, I see him lingering on deck, lost in thought.

Inscribed in a graceful feminine hand on the letter paper: "How are you? We are fine. Please do put your best effort into your duties. And let's both pray for peace."

The long-awaited letter from his mother. Among

shipmates who rejoice time and again upon receiving letters from home, he alone has never before known this happiness. He has reconciled himself to his sad fate: homeland and enemy country are one and the same.

Only one channel of communications remains open, via neutral Switzerland; yet at the very end, just before the fatal sortie, this letter has arrived.

Perhaps because of a limit on the number of words, the message is so simple. So straightforward.

"Let's both pray for peace." Loaded as it is with a thousand emotions, this line must have torn him wide open, he who had just come off duty translating American codes.

His mother's comforting, so true it hurts.

Wordless, I climb into my hammock.

4 April, early morning: a report that American planes attack. We take our stations.

Forenoon, afternoon: just as on the day before, we float at full alert, watching and waiting.

As we float, destroyer *Hibiki* hits a drifting mine and sends up a cloud of spray. The damage, though relatively slight, involves the boilers. *Hibiki* loses all way.

Of necessity, the decision is made to send *Hibiki* back to Kure under tow by sister ship *Hatsushimo*.

The two ships recede into the distance. From the decks of the remaining ships, seeing them off: glances of envy, sighs of grief.

From 1515 hours to 1915 hours, I am on duty as junior officer of the deck. Because we are on alert, I am not at my normal post at the gangway but on the bridge.

Junior officer of the deck, in charge of all discipline on board ship.

When I first came on board, a novice, an officer drafted out of college, I found a four-hour watch very demanding.

Without a moment's letup, one must maintain close watch over everything around the ship and keep an eye on the movement of the other ships at anchor; in addition, one must plan, implement, and inspect the daily schedule on board. The junior officer of the deck must always function on the double; walking will not do.

The captain voices his opinion about ways to improve morale: "Beginning tomorrow, even with the alert in force, we'll conduct comprehensive drills and extra physical conditioning exercises."

The emergency alert has been in force every day since we left Kure harbor, so it has been necessary to suspend the traditional intensive drills.

The five-day rest has restored the men's stamina to some degree, but it has not been enough to allow them to recover completely from endless days of overwork.

Still, we must guard against any letting up. The resumption of drills is an excellent way to enhance morale.

If the American task force attempts to keep us from getting underway, we must do our very best to counter it.

After dinner Rear Admiral Komura, commander of the Second Destroyer Squadron, comes on board from *Yahagi;* he confers with Vice Admiral Itō, commander in chief of Task Force II, whose flag is in *Yamato.* They will be going over particulars of the operation.

As became clear afterward, Admiral Itō, in command of Task Force II, from the outset expressed vigorous opposition to the concept of Operation *Ten'ichigo.* That strategy was being dictated in all particulars by Admiral Toyoda, commander in chief of the Combined Fleet, stationed permanently at Hiyoshi near Tokyo.

The first reason for Admiral Itō's opposition: the total absence of air cover. (The operation orders from Hiyoshi did not provide for a single friendly airplane.)

The second reason: the inferiority of our surface forces. (Our side had ten ships in all, including eight destroyers; the enemy had no fewer than sixty.)

The third: the delay in the time of sailing. (The orders set the time of getting underway at one day after the withdrawal of the American task force. Admiral Itō favored moving that up twelve hours, setting out cheek by jowl with the withdrawing American task force, and attacking at night on the high seas.)

Arguing that common sense would leave the final determination of time of sailing, if nothing else, to the officer in command on the scene, Admiral Itō reportedly gnashed his teeth in anger and indignation.

On board all is calm.

An order comes down from the communications staff officer. I am to take charge of a boat to carry documents to each of the vessels in the task force. They must be "rush" materials relating to the codes.

As I climb to the bridge, the night is dark and starless; on the distant shore, two flickering points of light, apparently fires from today's air raids.

2100 hours: looking to carry out my orders to the letter, I check on the charts the location of each anchored ship, wind direction and wind speed, and tides; I enter the information in my pocket notebook and hasten to the gangway.

Estimated time for the task: two and a half hours. The

boat to be used: my old friend *Daihatsu I* (wooden launch). Coxswain, the skillful Petty Officer Sugimoto.

Picking out the silhouette of the ship against a background black as lacquer, I grope my way toward the gangway.

What excellent training in getting to the lifeboat at night!

I remember. When I first came on board, day after day we devoted the hour before breakfast to practicing how to get to the lifeboats in the dim morning light. All in preparation for today.

Silent throughout, the coxswain and two crewmen go about the business of coming alongside and casting off.

The nine accompanying ships sit motionless on the black ocean. On board, now serenely asleep, 3,500 officers and men.

The launch makes one circuit of all the ships anchored in deployed formation, then hastens back to *Yamato*.

An alluring glow, light green, on the surface of the water. Plankton, floating in the launch's wake. A phosphorescent wave.

The aroma of the sea hangs in the night air.

Returning to *Yamato,* I report completion of the assignment to the communications staff officer. 2335 hours.

As I go up to the bridge, I can no longer make out a single point of light. Those fires on shore must have been put out.

In my quarters I set in order the record of the radar training. My desk is nearly concealed by the hammocks stretched between the beams. I sit at ease, almost on hands and knees, and let my pen race.

When I finish, I close my eyes for a moment.

The spring warmth is not far off. The spring I shall greet—will it be in this world?

I climb into my hammock and open a book.

Normally, because one drill follows another, no leisure exists for reading. But anticipating that we would have some free time at sea, I searched out a single volume in the ship's library below deck just before we sailed—a biography of the philosopher Spinoza. Most likely a personal copy left to the library by one of the ship's officers.

If we resume drills tomorrow, I won't have even a moment's leisure. I have read only a few pages, so there is no prospect that I can finish it before the attack.

So be it. I immerse myself in the book. The soft, almost novelistic style engulfs me like honey.

I remember. After I joined the navy, virtually every night for a month I was tormented by a nightmare: hungry for the printed word, I prowled bookstores, scanning with bloodshot eyes the titles on the spines of books I would never get to read.

5 April, forenoon: an inquiry from the gunnery officer concerning the particulars of the radar target exercises.

Yahagi is to tow the target, but what should the range be, and how long should the tow cable be?

The exercises are designed to calibrate the radar: *Yahagi* tows a target of metal screen, which reflects ultrashortwaves well; we make our observations simultaneously by radar and by visual rangefinder and azimuth compass, correlating for distance and bearing.

In conformity with yesterday's order from the captain, each division on ship resumes drills.

The general damage control training is the toughest.

The captain points out each and every failing and makes us repeat the drills over and over again.

Officers and men are still not in peak form. The bridge overflows with scathing criticism, with menace.

That we should still need to be driven like this right up to the very end!

Still, how to reconcile my awareness that we are not yet ready with my conviction that we must win?

What is it, anyway, this conviction that we must win?

Don't get sidetracked. This will be a rare trial by fire. When the moment of attack comes, just give it our best.

Afternoon: a report that the American task force is withdrawing as expected.

Has the time finally come?

An announcement from general headquarters concerning the progress of fighting on Okinawa. The American forces are steadily expanding their gains.

We have counted on Okinawa to be our last and strongest outpost; but if things proceed like this, it is only a matter of time before it too falls.

The loss of Okinawa will mean that the decisive battle, on the main islands, is at hand. But even if we cry out that it is the decisive battle, on the main islands, our present military strength allows us no prospect of success.

What does the future hold for us? Only certain defeat?

In our breasts, a flame burns. The mission assigned this operation—how crucial it is!

A break between drills. A voice cries out, "Cherry blossoms!" It is a member of the watch at the third station.

He has turned toward the coastline the mounted binoculars the watch uses; eyes to the eyepiece, he has raised his hand in excitement.

Must be an early-flowering variety.

Pushing to be next in line, we grasp the binoculars, seeking to engrave the delicate blossoms, petal by petal, on our retinas.

So bright and splendid, filling the hazy field of the binoculars; trembling unceasingly, enticing us.

Cherry blossoms, oh cherry blossoms of Japan—farewell!

1500 hours: the orders for sailing, sent from the commander in chief of the Combined Fleet to the commander in chief of Task Force II. Communicated to all those of junior-officer rank and above: "*Yamato* and the Second Destroyer Squadron will sally forth in a naval special attack via Bungo Channel at dawn of Day Y-minus-1; at dawn of Day Y they will charge into the seas west of Okinawa and will attack and destroy the enemy's invasion fleet. Day Y will be 8 April."

They say the admiral's earlier consultation with Rear Admiral Komura resulted in a decision to express determined opposition to this operation; has the opposition of the front-line unit been rejected out of hand?

In the first wardroom (the gunroom, cabin of the ensigns and lieutenants junior grade), debate heats up over the relative merits of battleships and airplanes.

No one maintains that battleships are superior.

An ironic voice asks: "Which country showed the world what airplanes could do by sinking *Prince of Wales?*"

At the time *Yamato* was designed, ten long years ago,

17

one could boast of the impregnability of her defenses. But it is unreasonable to think *Yamato* can maintain that impregnability in the face of rapid progress in the technology of aerial torpedoes and bombs, in the face of overwhelming numbers of torpedoes and bombs.

We have nothing to rely on but our very highest degree of readiness and our determined fighting spirit.

The Night before the Mission

1730 hours: over the ship's P.A.—
"All cadets, prepare to leave the ship."
"Distribute *saké* to all divisions."
"Open the ship's store." This order signals the beginning of festivities.

The first stage of preparations for sailing?

Arrangements for debarking the cadets go very quickly. Once these are completed, the cadets are summoned to the first wardroom. We exchange glasses of *saké* in ceremonial farewell.

Even though they came on board barely two days ago, eager about their new assignments, they have long lives ahead. We couldn't bear to take them along on an expedition into certain death.

Moreover, fifty newcomers would diminish our fighting strength, not augment it.

This time around, their departure from the ship cannot be avoided. Despite their long-cherished desire to serve in *Yamato*.

They had all begged to stay on board but had finally yielded to the executive officer's persuasion.

"Give it everything you've got! Do your part, and ours

too!" Their cries overlapping, they do the honors, pouring the *sake*.

How can we respond to their entreaty?

Raising his glass in toast, assistant navigator Ensign Suzuki (O.C.S.) loses his grip on it; it falls to the deck, shattering into a thousand pieces.

They say it is most unlucky to break the glass with which one toasts a departure.

He pales and is crestfallen; there is nothing he can do.

Our scornful glances pour in on him immediately— on the eve of departure, why should omens have frightened us?

And what were we relying on, those of us who held him in contempt?

How did we maintain our calm?

In fact, weren't we deluding ourselves that our own deaths would have the honor due the chosen few?

Imagining that we would die spectacular deaths in a suicide attack, weren't we clinging to the excitement of the extraordinary?

Or finding ourselves on a path offering no escape from certain death, weren't we intoxicated by the empty dream that we alone would return alive?

We deceived ourselves.

What awaited us was death and nothing else. Death, beyond a doubt.

No matter how splendid its raiment, death is death.

Were we prepared to accept a death from which all color had faded?

Only Ensign Suzuki had gone beyond illusion and faced up to his own death.

Look it straight in the face! Don't deceive ourselves!

Our wineglasses have all shattered. It is only for this short while, with great effort, that we grasp them with both hands.

Death is already nearby. Nothing stands in its way.

Meet death face to face!

Death: it can stand truth.

Let this opportunity slip and you'll have no chance to do a final reckoning of your short life, your lifetime of twenty-two years.

Ah, what a coward!

Deadening your senses now by taking refuge in alcohol.

Cloaking yourself in barbaric valor and false pride, laughing at your fellow officer who fears death.

Ensign Eguchi, watch officer, is in charge of order and shipboard routine. Even with the festivities about to begin, he still brandishes his swagger stick and reprimands the sailors for the way they enter the wardroom.

The way they place their feet, their salutes, their speech, the sequence in which they arrive—he points out all the lapses, interminably. As a result, the sailors are most reluctant to enter.

Assailed by his angry voice, one older sailor makes the same foolish motions over and over. His dry eyes move hardly at all.

The older sailor's behavior is not what it should be; perhaps because he knows what fate holds in store for him tomorrow, he has lost his sense of purpose.

The swagger stick hisses as Ensign Eguchi strikes him on the buttocks. A dull slapping sound. The old sailor falls over sideways; his cheek, pale under his sunburn, rubs along the deck.

Ensign Eguchi, probably young enough to be the sailor's son. Is it zeal that suffuses his eager face? or childishness?

"That's enough, Ensign Eguchi!" A shout from Lieutenant (jg.) Tomoda (O.C.S.).

Ensign Eguchi's face turns completely crimson. Swagger stick ready in his hand, he confronts Lieutenant Tomoda.

Lieutenant Usubuchi, chief of the first wardroom, stands at his chair, steps over, and speaks: "Don't be silly, Eguchi. Take that sailor; return to your division and have a long drink together. Tonight's the last night, isn't it? For both of you? At this point there's no sense in being so strict. The sailors won't feel like doing their best for you."

Lieutenant Usubuchi, outstanding member of the naval academy's 71st class. The bravest man on board and an inspiration to the morale of the whole crew, yet he has a fine human touch and is fond of anecdotes about the lives of great men.

In my first days on board *Yamato*, I once was the target of Lieutenant Usubuchi's fist.

One night, having finished night training, I was hurrying along the passageway to my quarters. A sailor coming toward me turned to the left a dozen or so meters in front of me and disappeared into the passageway along the port side of the ship. There was no doubt that for several seconds at least his eyes had met mine. A clear violation of regulations—an offense that normally would call for five blows of the fist.

"Halt!" I roared. When he retraced his steps and ran

up to me, I saw he was a young signalman. Fearing punishment, shoulders trembling, he studied my face intently.

"You must have seen me before you made that turn."

"I did, sir."

"Then why didn't you salute?" He stared at me and bit his lip.

"You knew you had acted in poor form, yet you turned away. You undoubtedly felt bad about it afterwards. Right?"

"Yes, sir." He looked back at me dubiously.

"Saluting takes only a slight effort; it's the simplest of all acts.But if you don't do it, it leaves a bad taste. How foolish!"

"Yes, sir."

"From now on, even if it's only your superior's back that you see, try saluting simply because it's the thing to do. It doesn't take a whole lot of effort. And you'll always feel good about it."

"Aye, aye, sir." Creases appeared on one cheek, and his face twisted into a smile.

"If you've got that, now let's see a real salute."

He repeated a determined salute several times and ran off with a little skip.

"Halt!" I turned around: Lieutenant Usubuchi. Even as that thought registered, his fist landed a blow on my left cheek. Caught off guard, I reeled.

"Are there really officers who act that way—observing an infraction and yet not striking the guilty party?" Not red with anger but pale with tension, he stood very close. "I watched the whole thing. And I understand in a way what you said. You probably put yourself in his shoes and figured that this time persuasion would be more effective than a punch."

22

"That's right, sir. I thought it would be the right thing not only for me, but for the sailor too."

"Where do you think you are? Out in the civilian world?"

"No, sir, aboard a warship."

"On the battlefield, no matter how nice and understanding an officer you are, it won't work. You must be strong."

"With all due respect, sir, I don't think so." For a moment we glared at each other.

"There's something in what you say. I understand that—why not put the two to the test? When the shells are flying, which sailors will perform better, mine or yours? Won't your sailors misread you, thinking, 'That officer is a nice guy, so he won't make us run through this hail of bullets'? The true worth of a soldier becomes apparent only on the battlefield. Got that?"

After the party breaks up, I make the rounds of the living quarters of the various divisions. Heavy drinking, happy drinking.

Because the flammable materials have been offloaded, there are neither tables nor chairs on deck.

We spread mats all over the deck, sit down in circles, and one after another we entertain the others. Most of us sing traditional folk songs from our home districts.

Pouring cold *saké* with a splash into an enormous cup, we drink it off in one draught. I do the honors for each of the sixteen men under my direct command.

The mission is upon us. Should we deny ourselves even oceans of *saké?* Of course not.

The 3,000 men of the crew. All shipmates in battle, one in body and spirit.

In the passageway I encounter a seaman second class. Because he belongs to another division, we don't know each other. Perhaps because he is slightly tipsy, his ruddy face positively glows.

I return his salute as correctly as I am able given my state of intoxication; and just as I am about to pass him, it hits me—our tombs will be not far apart. Better, he and I will form a single corpse.

I have a strong impulse to throw my arm around his shoulder and say, "Hello, friend!" I restrain myself with difficulty.

When I return to the first wardroom and resume my guzzling, the captain appears with the executive officer, carrying in each hand a huge bottle of *sake*.

The fifty lieutenants junior grade and ensigns form a human fence around them, and there is no end to the boisterous singing and wild dancing.

We pat the splendid bald head of the captain. A few even give it a good rap.

The executive officer, rumpled in the scrimmaging, gets his jacket torn.

I lose sight of the two. Soon it is about 2300 hours.

Over the P.A. the executive officer himself gives the order to everyone on ship: "Today we've all had a good time, and that's very much as it should be. But an end to it now." His voice has an unusually affectionate tone.

Blood drains from our faces; cramps run along our shoulders and arms.

Scolding voices, angry voices fly out in all directions and echo off the bulkheads.

I am befuddled with drink, and that ache in my breast is completely stilled.

6 April, 0000 hours: two destroyers come alongside, one to port and one to starboard, and begin the refueling operation. It takes hard work on the part of the entire engine room crew.

At the same time, we continue off loading all nonessentials.

In the bright moonlit night, a sense of expectancy pervades the ship.

About 0100 hours: a single B-29 passes directly over Yamato.

"Continue refueling, but man antiaircraft batteries." The plane is much too high, so we do not fire.

The tenacity with which this ship is being reconnoitered is enough to make us gnash our teeth.

Day after day the American reconnaissance planes have come in a diligent effort to capture Yamato's movements. And they have not missed the golden opportunity offered by this refueling for the mission.

0200 hours: the cadets finally leave the ship. Their transfer to a destroyer alongside is completed.

Running across the gangplank, they turn, look up at Yamato's bridge towering over them, and salute for a long moment.

They have long dreamed of becoming members of Yamato's crew; yet at this last moment before the mission, they must surrender that dream.

Twenty-odd sailors who recently have received orders reassigning them to other posts similarly cross the gangplank to the destroyer. "It's really a shame to leave the ship just before the mission." Even when their eyes are filled in fact with regret, one can detect in their words a relief at their narrow escape from the tiger's jaws.

A dozen or so sailors, seriously ill and not capable of performing battle duties, leave the ship accompanied by medical staff.

What to do with the older sailors, those over forty? In battle terms they are virtually ineffective. Moreover, in most cases their death in battle would be an enormous blow to their dependents.

The young officers take counsel among themselves. Based on these two considerations they recommend to the captain that these men leave the ship. They select from each division those who qualify and put forward a list of names.

After consulting his staff, the captain permits some of these men to leave the ship.

The offloading of all nonessentials is finished. The readying of *Yamato* for battle proceeds apace.

While all is still dark, the refueling comes to an end, and the destroyers on either side pull away.

They had rushed about the two bases, Kure and Tokuyama, collecting the fuel they have loaned us to replenish our supplies. Thanks to this arduous stopgap measure, all our ships have received the fuel they need.

But from now on, won't the ships remaining in the Inland Sea run out of fuel?

Three B-29s pass directly overhead. They must have verified that the refueling operation is over.

The Morning of the Sortie

Early morning: the ship's P.A.—"We will get under way at 1600 hours." "All hands assemble on the foredeck

26

at 1800 hours." Charged with eagerness, the voice of the officer on duty roars over the P.A. system.

The day of the mission has come.

Once more we check that hatches, doors, and covers have been sealed.

The work of getting ready is almost completed. In the midst of growing tension on board, all remains calm.

Time hangs heavy.

The ship's P.A.: "The deadline for mail is 1000 hours." Even though we are in no mood for it, we all encourage each other and try to write home.

How difficult to write a letter to be read after one's death! But I must requite those kind enough to hope for even a single word written by me.

What to do about mother's grief?

Is there any way that I, unfilial in dying ahead of her, can now console her?

Can anyone take my place in shouldering her grief? No.

Nor is there any method of communicating to her my gratitude that my whole life has been the gift of her love.

No. Chin up.

What is left inside me is a battle, nothing more. I am a warrior about to take the field, nothing more.

Don't picture her bent over in grief.

Encouraging myself in this way, I finally write:

"Please dispose of all my things. Please, everyone, stay well and survive. That is my only prayer." What more can I say?

My parting emotions are clear in the letter; she will grieve for me.

I can only submit and die. I can only hope that my death will bear fruit.

Rejoice, mother, if I am lucky enough to die a death of which I need not be ashamed.

Emotions that touch the very heart of the reader: I am not up to rereading the letter. I hurry to the mail box, stuff the letter in, and escape from my quarters.

Thus are severed all bonds tying me to my own flesh and blood.

Why is it that even at this moment my father's grief is so little in my thoughts? Only for a moment does my memory summon up the rather lonely sight of his back as he drinks his evening *saké*.

Ensign Suzuki, a solicitous man, asks each of his shipmates: "Already written your letter?"

If someone turns his face away: "What? Not yet? Don't you *have* a mother? Even a single word will do, so write." Pressing the man, he places a pen in his hand.

The ensigns and lieutenants junior grade gather in the first wardroom and receive our allotment of cigarettes, which are ceremonial gifts from the emperor, and ship's store items. An abundance of candy, tiny bottles of whiskey, soda. It barely fits into the two pockets of our uniforms.

A few men on duty as lookouts or as navigators must take their stations earlier than the rest of us. Each wraps his last clean uniform in a pure white carrying cloth. Swords in hand, they stand at the door, heels together, nod silently, then turn smartly and leave. Our last view of them.

"Do a good job!" "Die a death worthy of you!" The parting words of fellow officers, seeing them off. Their shoulders are already squared; in response to such brave parting words, their shoulders become squarer still.

This is the final parting of comrades in arms who are as close to one another as blood relatives, yet no one slaps shoulders or shakes hands. Simple and silent nods, no more.

Flowing beneath these brief nods: emotions that would do justice to the most painful of leavetakings.

I go to the sailors' bunkroom. Many are writing final letters. Seaman first class Hashimoto, who is under my direct command, gets up from his cot and salutes.

At his feet, atop several sheets of stationery written on in pencil, I see a memorial lock of hair. Forty years old, he has four children; in civilian life he is a greengrocer. A pleasant fellow, but his performance record is poor.

According to what a noncommissioned officer said later, just before the mission Seaman Hashimoto got together all his things, down to the last sheet of paper, and mailed them home. Among the older sailors, quite a few were like him.

Two B-29s fly over, one after the other: high-altitude reconnaissance. Are the American forces already intent on predicting the hour of our sailing?

The Operation Commences

Afternoon: we prepare to sail. It is a sailing that holds no promise of a return.

A seaplane has landed near the gangway.

We store our battle kits at our designated battle stations. The upper radar compartment, near the top of the main tower and directly under the bridge. 110 rungs up the ladder from the deck, at a height of 33 meters above the water.

29

From now on, no matter what happens, we are not to leave our posts.

The radar equipment functions very smoothly.

That seaplane circles over the task force, then flies off to the east.

The battleship's flag flutters atop the main tower.

Yamato is now ready for battle.

Basking in the honor of taking part in her final sortie: the 3,332 men of the crew.

1600 hours. We get under way. "All engines, ahead one-third."

Task force course: 120 degrees.

Flagship: *Yamato.* On board, Vice Admiral Itō Seiichi, commander of Task Force II.

Escort: the nine ships of the Second Destroyer Squadron. Cruiser *Yahagi* and destroyers *Fuyutsuki, Suzutsuki, Yukikaze, Isokaze, Hamakaze, Hatsushimo, Asashimo, Kasumi.* All are crack ships, tempered in a hundred battles.

The final task force sortie of the Japanese navy. Ten picked vessels—the best.

At this moment, each of the other ships conducts a simulated attack, treating *Yamato* as an enemy ship. They perform flawlessly.

Spread out in circular formation with *Yamato* in the center, we make straight for Bungo Channel at base speed (12 knots), deliberately.

Destroyers *Hanazuki, Kaya,* and *Maki,* which preceded us here from Tokuyama as an anti-submarine unit, turn back and head for home.

Full of spirit and biting through the pure white crests of the waves: our escort ships.

The arrow has been loosed.

By turns we stand lookout duty. I am the lookout officer.

My place of duty is in the middle of the bridge, the heart and brains of the ship; my duty is to supervise the lookouts stationed at sixteen places on board and to evaluate their reports, deciding which to pass on to the staff officers, from the captain on down. When we are steaming on alert, it is a most important duty.

Two meters to my right, the commander in chief (a vice admiral). One meter to my left, the chief of staff (a rear admiral). Considering that I'm a novice O.C.S. man, I'm pretty lucky to be here.

Yamato advances inexorably, throwing up a bow wave to either side.

Thanks to the incomparable seaworthiness of the ship's construction, there is no pitch or roll; even on the bridge, we have the illusion of standing on firm ground.

This very moment our ten ships push onward with single purpose, defying the currents.

1800 hours: we muster at quarters. Clean uniforms.

This is probably the final muster. Soon after being dismissed, we will go to our battle stations. There will be no occasion for another muster.

We can look forward only to demonstrations of unity and strength at each battle station.

Because the operation is already under way, the captain cannot leave the bridge.

In his place the executive officer passes on the words of farewell addressed to the task force by the commander in chief of the Combined Fleet:

"This task force of the Imperial Navy, in cooperation with the army, is about to stake its entire air, sea, and land might on an all-out attack against enemy ships in the vicinity of Okinawa.

"The fate of the empire hangs in the balance.

"For this occasion we have organized a naval special attack task force and have given it orders for an attack unparalleled in its heroic bravery. We have done this to exalt the glorious tradition of the surface forces of the Imperial Navy, gathering together the might of the Imperial Navy for this one battle, and to transmit its glory to posterity.

"Let each unit, special attack unit or no, fight fiercely, annihilate the enemy task force at every turn, and thereby make secure for all eternity the foundations of the empire."

Well said.

Bows in the direction of the emperor. The singing of the national anthem.

Military songs. Each ship responds to the others as if in echo.

Three shouts of *banzai*.

Looming high above us in the bright moonlight, the main tower. Indescribable.

We are dismissed. I am about to climb down the hatch on the starboard side of main battery 1 when I notice an officer lingering on the foredeck.

The face seen from the side in the clear moonlight, the shadow of the bushy eyebrow falling on the cheek, is that of Ensign Mori.

He who is noted for having the greatest capacity for drink of anyone on board, for being broadminded, and for having a beautiful fiancée. That lovely face in the photograph that never leaves his person and those beautiful and clear brush strokes of the letters he receives regularly are the envy of the entire first wardroom.

I understand that one night just before he was due to be called up into O.C.S., he grasped her hand for the first time and with these brief words made his farewell: "Your eyes, your mouth, your nose, your hands and feet—they all belong to me."

He turns on me the gaze he had been directing at the dark waves and speaks close to my ear, as if pleading.

"I'll be dead, so I'm no problem. Those who die will be the lucky ones. No problem with me. But what about her? How to get her to be happy?

"A better man than I will surely show up, marry her, and make her happier than I could. That's how it will be, I'm sure.

"Her happiness with me is already over. I'm bound now for death. So I want her to find some greater happiness. Marry a nicer fellow. Accept that new happiness without reservation.

"I'll die leaving behind one who will truly grieve for me. I'm a lucky one. But what will become of her, left behind? She'll make a good marriage and be happy. I hope for that, for that alone. When she's truly happy again, that's when I'll live on in her, live on . . .

"But how can I get that wish of mine across? I've told her repeatedly in person. And I've written it in letters any number of times. 'Find a greater happiness with someone else—that alone is my final wish.' . . . But how can I make sure? What guarantee do I have that she'll comply?

"Shall I pray? My resolve is so real that I can't help praying. But is that alone enough? If I prostrate myself and pray, will that do it? Cry out from the depths of my soul:

33

'Somehow, please, let her hear my plea!'—is that all I can do?"

His tone is gruff; there are no tears. He pours out his intense entreaty. No, his anger.

He spitting out his anger. I nodding, speechless. Over our heads, the clear moonlit night we are seeing for the last time.

Beneath our feet, the stout foredeck we will not set foot on again.

You, his intended. You had won a love without equal.

You should heed the prayer into which he poured his whole being. You must heed it.

Still angry, he breaks off and stares intently at the waves beneath our feet.

On the surface of the jet-black sea, silver-white crests of waves that shatter and vanish.

My eyes blur with tears, and I turn away. The wind blowing across my cheeks is cool.

Good old Ensign Mori will die tomorrow giving a fine account of himself.

He stands stock-still even as I slap him on the shoulder. I run to the hatch and hurry down the ladder.

The die is cast. The mission leads to certain death. We can do nothing about it now.

Praying, praying fervently, he will die; in the end she will do as he prays. It can be no other way.

I run on, for some reason so impatient, so exasperated that I seem to drive my feet through the deck.

I go straight to my post and turn my thoughts to the enemy.

The task force has increased speed to twenty knots.

On the bridge I listen to talk about the mission.

Our mission is connected inseparably with our special attacks against the American landing zones on Okinawa and is coordinated also with the army's counterattacks on land; it constitutes one facet of Operation *Kikusui,* which calls for an all-out air assault.

The special attack planes, overloaded with explosives (most carry a payload of a ton and a half) are far too slow; there is real concern that they will fall easy prey to the American fighter planes. Moreover, in this Okinawa operation a fierce counterattack by American planes is inevitable, so there is a very strong likelihood that the special attacks will miscarry.

That being the case, it is deemed wise to have *Yamato* act for the duration as decoy to draw off the swarm of American interceptors and weaken those defenses. Still, to be good bait we must not only be attractive enough as a target to draw off most of the enemy forces but must have the antiaircraft defenses to resist for many hours.

Yamato has been chosen as the decoy best meeting these criteria. To prolong her life even further, an escort of nine ships has been assigned.

An assault against Okinawa is only ostensibly our objective. Our real aim is to become the target of a concentrated attack by the crack American task force.

Hence all ships have only enough fuel for the voyage there. Returning is simply not in the plans.

Yamato's 46 centimeter guns, vaunted as the world's largest and armed with a full supply of shells, stand ready and eager. But their mission is to be a decoy, no more. There is barely enough fuel for a one-way trip.

Bravery? Recklessness?

Needless to say, a plan has also been drawn up for the highly unlikely event that *Yamato* actually reaches the landing zones on Okinawa. That plan calls for *Yamato*'s main batteries to shell the American forces already landed on Okinawa.

Of the full load (1,200 rounds) of ammunition, the armor-piercing shells are to be used to destroy the support ships and the type-3 antiaircraft shells to inflict casualties.

The armor-piercing shells, weighing 3,000 pounds each, are used to sink enemy ships. They have great power to penetrate. Those that strike the water send up geysers 150 meters high. The type-3 shells, which have timed fuses and explode into fragments, normally are used to shoot down planes. Their range is thirty kilometers, and they break into 6,000 pieces that scatter in all directions. One volley once brought down an entire formation of ten planes.

The broad outlines of the operation are as follows. First, all ships will charge ahead, attract the American naval and air forces, and open the way for the success of the special attack planes. Any ship still afloat will simply press forward into the very midst of the enemy until she runs aground; all hands will fight with might and main until all ammunition is expended. Then any men still alive with one bound will become footsoldiers and join the fray. Hence machine guns and pistols have been distributed to each division.

Never in the annals of naval warfare has there been such a special attack, nor will there ever be another.

According to the explanation offered after the war by those responsible, this operation was decided upon against all common sense because of increasing difficulty in maintaining this giant ship, which devoured as much oil as thirty destroyers; because of exasperation due to the imminence of defeat; and because of concern for the prestige of the surface forces vis-à-vis the *kamikaze* special attack planes.

36

The statement seemed to imply considerable remorse at the loss of six fine ships and the lives of several thousand men.

Even taking all such conditions into account, this operation clearly was too crude, too imprudent.

Given the stubborn opposition of the entire staff of Task Force II, from Admiral Itō on down, and of the captain of each ship, naval headquarters recognized that the situation was so extraordinary that only personal persuasion had any prospect of success. The decision was reached to dispatch as special envoy Admiral Kusaka, chief of staff of the Combined Fleet, a classmate of Admiral Itō at the naval academy and his close friend.

The seaplane that flew in just before we sailed carried Admiral Kusaka's party.

Admiral Kusaka had taken part in the deliberations over the plans for this operation. He called the task force's entire staff together on board *Yamato* and offered the following explanation of the aims of the operation: At this moment when the survival of the nation stands at a crossroads, nothing is more satisfying to us as warriors than to be able to bring into play this last ornament of our surface forces, this strong right arm made ready by long years of arduous effort.

That decision having been made, so long as bullets fly we wish to repay at least a tiny fraction of our indebtedness to the emperor by fighting furiously, each man a match for thousands, and by annihilating the enemy down to his last warship and last vessel, thus restoring our momentum at one fell swoop.

Yet even though the task force's duty as a naval special attack force is so important, the makeup of the task force is irregular, and it has not had sufficient training since the last personnel changes. Therefore it is hoped that those at all levels of command will strive to ascertain the capabilities of those under their command and will go about their tasks carefully and boldly, with superhuman effort in matters of command, thus eliciting the utmost fighting strength from each ship.

The main purpose of this operation lies in the mortal attack to be delivered by the land-based airplanes; but because the enemy's military strength is colossal, we must expect to engage an enemy task force superior to our own. The normal tactic against a superior enemy task force would be a night attack; but with the recent advances in radar, even a night attack on this enemy is not to be taken lightly. A dispersed attack at night, feints with part of the force, decoying with an oblique two-stage attack: such tactics call for detailed preparations and study; and for the blow to be decisive the main force must lead a concerted attack the next morning. Thus Admiral Kusaka.

Admiral Itō's doubts focused on the issue of the "real objective of the operation" behind the rhetorical flourishes of the orders; he was won over at last only after receiving the final word—"you are being requested to die gloriously, heralding the deaths of 100,000,000 Japanese who prefer death to surrender."

Once again, Admiral Itō straightened his shoulders and asked, "What of the end of this operation? In case we incur extensive damage on the way in, will the decision as to how to deal with that situation be left to me?" Admiral Kusaka replied, "In the past we have often been remiss in not letting the commanding officer on the scene take action on his own authority. We want you to plan ahead of time in your own mind, so that without waiting for orders you will be able to do what is best in light of the overall plan and in response to changing conditions. Of course, the staff at headquarters too has prepared plans against an emergency."

The young captain of one of the destroyers grilled Admiral Kusaka's entourage: if, as the parting words of the chief of staff of the Combined Fleet indicate, the power of the Imperial Navy is really to be marshaled for this one battle, "then why doesn't Admiral Toyoda himself venture out from his bunker at Hiyoshi and assume direct command?" He was voicing the innermost thoughts of the entire crew of this special attack task force.

What are the prospects for Operation *Ten'ichigo?* The vehement debate among the officers continues.

Those arguing that it can only fail are in the overwhelming majority.

The confluence of various conditions foreseeable when *Yamato* sails:

The American reconnaissance, unprecedented in its thoroughness;

The huge and powerful task force that, our intelligence confirms, is waiting for us in the vicinity of Okinawa;

The critical disparity in naval air power, unprecedented in large battles on the high seas.

In addition: doubts about the time of sailing and the course;

That we will be as vulnerable as a man walking alone on a dark night carrying only a lantern;

That we will be hit by submarines as soon as we enter Bungo Channel;

Or that midway we will fall victim to airborne torpedoes. (This prediction, subscribed to by a large number of the young officers, will prove to be precisely on the mark.)

Against this sharp contention that the mission is doomed to fail, chief officer of the watch Lieutenant Usubuchi (chief of the first wardroom), binoculars fixed on the sea at dusk, speaks in a low voice, almost a whisper:

"The side which makes no progress never wins. To lose and be brought to one's senses: that is the supreme path.

"Japan has paid too little attention to progress. We have been too finicky, too wedded to selfish ethics; we have forgotten true progress. How else can Japan be saved except by losing and coming to its senses? If Japan does not come to its senses now, when will it be saved?

"We will lead the way. We will die as harbingers of Japan's new life. That's where our real satisfaction lies, isn't it?"

Lieutenant Usubuchi's firmly held opinion becomes the general conclusion of the serious discussion continuing day after day in the wardroom. No one is able to refute it.

As indications grow that the sortie is imminent, the pervasive anguish and distress of the younger officers cannot but give rise to many arguments.

It is already impossible to conceal the fact that this task force will be vanquished, that final defeat of Japan is simply a matter of time—but defeat for what reason? defeat under what conditions?

What is more, we who stand in the front line are already on the brink of death—but death to what end? death to pay for what? death how recompensed?

Those ensigns and lieutenants junior grade who graduated from the naval academy speak as if with one voice: "We die for the nation, for the emperor. Isn't that enough? Do we need anything more than that? Can't we die content with that?"

An O.C.S. man colors and asks in return: "We die for sovereign and country. I understand that. But isn't there more to it than that? My death, my life, the defeat of Japan as a whole: I'd like to link all these with something more general, more universal, something to do with values. What the devil is the purpose of all this?"

"That's nonsense. That's a useless argument, a dangerous argument. Isn't it enough to wear on your breast the chrysanthemum emblem of the special attack force and to die with 'long live the emperor' on your lips?"

"If that's all there is, I don't like it a bit. There has to be something more."

In time it turns into a rain of fists, a free-for-all. "Okay, we'll have to thrash that rottenness out of you."

The position expressed by Lieutenant Usubuchi succeeds, just before the mission, in restraining the debate and saving the situation.

Entering Hostile Waters

At long last the vanguard of the task force is about to reach midchannel.

From here on we will be in hostile waters. To starboard, Kyūshū; to port, Shikoku; yet the enemy controls the sea, controls the sky.

The ships are deployed in a formation used for sailing at night under submarine threat: *Yamato* in the center and *Yahagi* bringing up the rear, and 2,500 meters separating each ship from the next.

We begin radar watch for submarines. It will be conducted the whole night through.

Fight with all our might: that is all we can do.

I go to the upper radar compartment. Steamy from the heat of the equipment, it is heavy with the odors of humanity.

Four off-duty sailors sleep, piled up in a dark corner.

How many hours of life do their bodies have left? A few? a dozen or so at the outside?

Moldering like mud, they sleep, oblivious. Is their exhaustion already so severe?

When I enter the instrument compartment, four men on duty are conducting a thorough search for contacts. They are calm, no different from the way they are during a drill.

This ship's radar plot governs the movements of the other nine ships. Every movement of these men controls the entire task force from moment to moment.

Now the consecutive days and nights of hard training are paying off.

The vitality that fills their bodies, the cheerful confidence so apparent in their faces. Fortunate ones, they.

Listening, they detect on two different bearings what appear to be American submarines. When they turn our radar to these bearings, they also get weak contacts.

First, they pick up in the receivers the transmissions sent out by the American radar; then they confirm their finding by sending out transmissions intermittently in the same direction.

If we transmit first, we inevitably reveal our position; by doing it this way we hope to ascertain the movement of the enemy while keeping him from ascertaining ours.

Two submarines? Three? Apparently the ones that have been in contact all along.

We repeatedly take urgent evasive action dictated by the positions of the enemy submarines.

Because it is nighttime, optical instruments are virtually useless. All we can do is turn our hydrophones in those directions and get ready for the sound of torpedoes being fired.

If we hear that sound, we can plot their course from the intensity, direction, and speed of the sound and try to dodge them.

Submarines, appearing so soon, in midchannel. Even judging only from their skillful and quick shadowing, it is clear that the American offensive is no ordinary one.

We must be ready to be the target of torpedoes coming from all directions.

The intelligence unit in charge of monitoring enemy communications intercepts an urgent radio communication from an American submarine to the flagship of the task force and to U.S. Pacific headquarters on Guam.

It is not in code, but in plain language. Do the Americans hold us in contempt? Or is code unnecessary because the contents are not much of a secret?

"Enemy task force headed south. At least one battleship and many destroyers. Course 190 degrees, speed 25 knots . . ." Moment by moment, they report our progress in detail.

"I do believe we learn about our position faster from their side than from ours!" The navigation officer, with a wry smile.

Even though anticipated, it startles us that the tracking is so thorough.

2345 hours. Fifteen minutes before I go on duty on the bridge.

When I go on duty, I will relieve the chief radar officer, Lieutenant (jg.) Ōmori; on the bridge I will report the radar situation to the staff officers.

Because this task is the focal point of the nighttime watch against submarines, it is more than enough responsibility for me.

Pushing open the curtain that shuts off the radar room, I climb the ladder to the bridge, one step at a time. The fierce wind hits me.

Dark clouds veil the moon, hide the moon; the night becomes darker still. Not one point of light in my range of vision, only unending darkness.

Toyed with by the wind, my body flattens against the ladder like a sheet of paper.

Wait! Say a last prayer here for those at home. A fine opportunity. Fail to make use of it, and there won't be another.

If even a single person were to observe me, the sanctity of the moment would be profaned. My heart would not be in it.

But when tomorrow's sun rises, it will already be too late. Glad I realized that now. Thank goodness.

Orienting myself according to the ship's compass course and turning to face what I presume to be the direction of home, I grip the handrail tightly and bow my head.

The rivets of the rail are icy against my palms, but inside my body I feel a flush of warmth.

Father, mother, older sister, late brother-in-law lost in action a year ago. They stand clearly before me.

And the faces of acquaintances, teachers, and friends pass before my mind's eye and fade.

People I have met in my short life and cannot forget: their images blanket my sight, and I pay my respects to them as if they really stood in front of me.

They are colorless apparitions, but when they smile desolately, I recognize their faces.

"I am grateful to you," I whisper repeatedly, instinctively.

Your kindness in forgiving me for being as willful as a baby, in giving me companionship.

I have gained the road to an easy death. Death is easy.

You not blessed with death, you who are still forced to live. How will you endure all the days after tomorrow?

The hardships of those days are beyond my comprehension.

Fleeing alone from having to endure them, I really deserve nothing from you, but please permit me to hope for one beam of light on my path.

That you will have joys in the future. That you will have the blessings of a new life.

Never underestimate how precious life is . . .

I must not immerse myself too long in such thoughts.

I raise my head and climb, holding onto the rail; a sudden gust of wind blows up and from the side thrusts me in through the entrance to the bridge.

The bridge is of course under blackout. In the dim half-light there is high tension.

There is virtually no movement; the figures are frozen, as in a shadow play.

Each is rooted to his assigned post and engrossed in his duty. A pleasant sense of fulfillment prevails.

Officers, junior officers, sailors, twenty in all.

"Such-and-such degrees, such-and-such. . . .": the reports of direction and distance from the radar. "Nothing new": the reports from the sonar. Only these voices shatter the silence.

For convenience in nighttime identification, fluorescent dots have been attached to the back of each cap.

For the commander in chief, one dot; for the captain, two; for the executive officer, three—their pale glow illuminates the area immediately around them; if they move ever so slightly, the sight is as beautiful as points of light in a dream, bringing smiles to our lips.

We are about to do battle. We are about to do battle. Tomorrow is the day of the battle.

We must fight single-mindedly, with no second thoughts.

We receive a message from the chief of staff of the Combined Fleet: our special attacks are inflicting heavy damage on the enemy task force in the vicinity of Okinawa.

No reaction from any of the staff officers on the bridge.

We advance into a region where we can navigate close to shore. We have made it this far without hearing the sound of torpedoes.

The American submarines have confined themselves to scouting us, perhaps because they plan an all-out attack on the high seas. They have fired no torpedoes.

This is almost more than we could have hoped for.

As we approach Kyūshū with its high rocky coast and deep offshore waters, we shift to navigation close to shore. Against submarines at night, it is the safest course, confining their attack to one side and making it difficult to get our range and bearing by radar.

Column formation: *Yahagi* in the van, *Yamato* in the rear.

We institute a condition-two alert. This cuts in half the number of men on watch and enables them to rest by turns.

A dark night. Visibility is very poor. To guard against

running aground we use our radar to calculate the distance from ship to shore and proceed, hugging the coast as closely as possible.

With *Yamato*'s radar, the margin of error is less than fifty meters.

Until we attack, everything must be this careful and exact. A precious vessel.

Yamato is of course our principal offensive and defensive force.

I report our distance from shore moment by moment. How great this responsibility! With bated breath, I check my rising excitement.

Morning on the High Seas

7 April, dawn. We pass through Ōsumi Strait. In circular formation we continue west, *Yamato* at the center and a distance of 1,500 meters between ships.

Of the six Zero seaplanes *Yamato* normally carries for purposes of reconnaissance, we left five in Kure; now we catapult the remaining plane aloft and send it back to a base at Kagoshima. If we kept it here, the plane would have little chance of escaping the sad fate of going to the bottom of the sea.

In accordance with operation orders, the sky above the task force holds no friendly aircraft to defend us.

In the face of the powerful American reconnaissance forces, certain to have swung into action immediately after we did, the naval special attack task force is stripped of all air support.

From now on we will see no friendly aircraft.

47

Some people think that even the support of two hundred or three hundred fighter planes would have virtually no effect against the overwhelming and furious attack of a total of 1,000 planes.

On the new carriers like *Amagi* and *Katsuragi,* waiting at Kure, rumors flared that they were now to go into operation.

Had they in fact put to sea, the best crews and fighter planes in the Kure area would have been annihilated, and with nothing to show for it.

Twenty reconnaissance planes, sent up contrary to mission orders on the responsibility of the base commander at Kanoya, were reconnoitering some tens of miles ahead of the task force, though we did not know it. Soon after sunrise, they broke radio contact with the base and, still in that state, were engulfed by a swarm of planes of the American combat air patrol. Having lost more than half their number, they headed for home.

Admiral Itō's only son, a flight officer, was on duty as a member of one of the first-line crews. The admiral must surely have foreseen that chances were good his son would take part in the operation.

Indeed, it may have been his long-cherished desire that when the country's doom became imminent father and son would take part together in a glorious suicide mission.

Fulfilling his father's expectations, Lieutenant (jg.) Itō took part in all the patrolling that was part and parcel of Operation *Ten'ichigo* and fortunately returned alive; but ten days later he flew to his death on Okinawa as a member of the *Kikusui* special attack force.

The son tries to protect the father and then chooses the waters nearby as the site for his own valiant death.

Just at sunrise the submarines fade from our radar screens, and in their place reconnaissance planes begin to shadow us.

Submarines by night and planes by day: usual reconnaissance practice.

They pursue us, circling skillfully near the extreme range of antiaircraft fire of each ship in the task force.

If we see a chance and open fire, they duck the shots adroitly and then come in a bit closer to continue their pursuit.

Here stands revealed the disadvantage of having no air cover.

Ever since we sailed, they have had our every movement under observation.

What is more, the ceiling is low, and visibility around 10,000 meters is very poor; more than once we lose sight of the planes tracking us. Not to mention the fact that it is impossible to locate the enemy task force early on.

Weather conditions are extremely adverse.

Flying above the task force a few planes at a time, formations of American fighter planes make repeated contact.

Martin flying boats also join in; this shadowing operation has been carefully thought out.

We begin antiaircraft radar search. At every moment reports come in on the range and bearing of the planes shadowing us. We know precisely where they are.

Still, how skillful their pursuit! Sometimes boldly, sometimes circumspectly, taking advantage of the weather conditions to duck in and out among the clouds, they maintain contact.

All ships are making twenty knots; at intervals of five minutes we execute evasive maneuvers.

All ships simultaneously carry out a complicated zig-zag, repeating the pattern every five minutes. Simply steaming straight ahead would reveal our course and make it easy for the waiting submarines to zero in on us. The zigzags conceal our course.

On the right wing of the formation, *Asashimo* suddenly begins to fall behind. She hoists signal flags: "Engine trouble."

Asashimo soon grows small in the distance; she radios us that urgent repairs are under way.

A follow-up message: "Repairs will take five hours."

Dropping out already? A grim premonition runs up my spine.

The bridge is calm, as usual. The movements of the staff officers and the sending and receiving of signals are quite brisk, but that is all.

The calm before the storm?

Breakfast.

Probably the last meal we can enjoy in a normal atmosphere.

I cannot bear to eat it inside this gloomy compartment. I scramble up the ladder outside the radar compartment, come out atop the platform of the antenna used in sending out transmissions, a flat area a little more than two meters square. I take a big bite out of my ball of rice.

An ideal spot, surrounded by sky. When the sea wind blows up and threatens to knock me off, I hold on by wrapping my legs around the support.

I cannot keep this wonderful spot all to myself. I summon Petty Officer Katahira, a skilled radar operator, and we eat together, our knees bumping.

He hurries through his meal silently and then departs with a stiff nod. His face betrays his impatience to be alone.

Thirty-three years old and noted for his thorough grasp of the theoretical aspects of radar and high skill in its practice, he has left a pregnant wife at home. What is more, this is their first child, eagerly awaited.

And yet father and child will never meet. The child will never feel its father's gaze; the father will die without having known his child's touch.

Nothing whatsoever can be done about it.

As his immediate superior, I censor his letters, and so I know all about the situation. And he knows that I know. Was he afraid that he was about to hear words of consolation from a superior officer younger than he, and single? That would have been too humiliating.

Had I been a fellow sailor struggling with the same thoughts, our consoling each other would have provided a moment of happiness.

Gloomy and finicky fellow. Should he die with his narrow-mindedness unchanged, he won't live on in his wife.

I didn't want to console you. I know I'm not the one for that. I wished only to enjoy with you this last morning and this cool, refreshing salt air.

I have no wife. No children, of course. Only my parents and sister will mourn my death.

I have not experienced the flames of love.

Facing death, I am not bound by any ties whose breaking would drive me frantic.

Petty Officer Katahira and I—which of us is the lucky one? which the unlucky?

Should I rest content that I am blessed with peace of mind, having only my own flesh and blood to mourn my death?

Or is the true meaning of life to be found in heartwrenching anguish like his?

My eyes, staring vacantly while I am absorbed in thought, itch for sleep and are hot. The cool breeze bathes my eyes in pain.

The morning sun, its dull yellow rays reflecting off the waves through gaps in the clouds, is dazzling but pleasant.

With a happy heart I wonder: since I was weaned from my mother's breast and came to savor the morning meal, how many thousands of times—how many tens of thousands of times—have I eaten breakfast?

Breakfast: after today breakfast and I will be utterly without connection. I shake my head in disbelief.

The sea is exceedingly blue; heavy waves strike the side of the ship.

The southernmost coast of Kyūshū is already fading from sight astern. These eyes will not see again the fields and hills of home.

Each moment they become more distant, and we are separating for good. Now not a single island is visible.

Task force course: 280 degrees. Roughly west-northwest.

Even though the main island of Okinawa lies to the southwest, we are scheduled to make a long detour, advancing on this course to the halfway point to conceal our intentions and to avoid the main body of the American task force.

Plan A called for an advance directly down the Ryūkūan archipelago; Plan B called for a slight detour; and Plan C, a wide detour. It is said that the discussion focused primarily on these three before Plan C was finally chosen.

The task force is strongly opposed. The situation is clearly dire, with no room for such tricks.

The best idea would be to proceed under cover of darkness at full speed straight for Okinawa.

We encounter a convoy of ships flying the Japanese flag. A convoy of several small transports.

Where are they returning from? They pass us, threading their way through our formation.

The hazy forms of the ships; their tired wakes. Sad, to think of the troubles they've experienced.

At long last they are almost home. But what sacrifices have they made to get back this far?

They signal to us in *Yamato:* "We pray for your success." Smiles fill the bridge.

To receive parting wishes from a bunch of decrepit old tubs like them! We reply promptly: "We will not disappoint you."

On the decks of the passing ships, no sailors wave goodbye. They encounter Japan's last task force sortie, yet they stay below deck.

How great their relief when they finally see the home islands close at hand!

On board each ship in the task force, eyes gazing after the transports as they fade in the distance. Eyes. A sense of desolation, so vivid it is almost hypnotic.

Asashimo recedes farther out of sight. If a lone ship drops out of the task force, the American planes will inevitably focus on it.

Something must be done. Urgent consultations.

A decision is made. At the point where we are to change course from west-northwest to south-southwest, we will steam back to *Asashimo*. Then, after reintegrating her into the formation, we will turn back once again onto the prescribed course.

Asashimo's damage is said to be to one part of her reduction gear.

About 0900 hours: I go to the upper radar compartment (surface radar).

Yamato's radar compartment happens to be off duty. The entire task force of ten ships is divided into two watches, and the two watches stand radar watch by turns.

Relieved from duty, the sailors sit mute at their posts.

Two older sailors squat, shoulders hunched, clouded eyes expressing bitterness. Their gazes fall fixed and unwavering to the deck.

Discipline no longer holds. Because death makes them bold? Or because death has ground them down to the point of exhaustion?

They are no longer men under military discipline. They are simply individual human beings.

What kicks in the pants, what whip on their backs, what words can call them to account for their poor form?

Are they lamenting that this, the last of their many pleasures, is being taken from them? Or weeping over the difficult days ahead for their wives and children?

I distribute cigarettes, the ceremonial gift from the emperor. I pass around a pocket-sized bottle of whiskey for a sip each. Our last chance to enjoy ourselves as a group.

Without even raising his head, Petty Officer Miyazawa reports: "The equipment is in first-rate condition, sir."

This mission caught him unawares, on the fourth day after his wedding.

"I'm thinking of getting married the next time we

54

have shore leave; I'd like your opinion, sir." He asked me that a month ago, when we were in the midst of intensive training in the home seas.

Having made sure of his prospective bride's home environment, her character, and how well they knew each other, I gave my approval immediately.

I knew that the mission was approaching, but I never thought it would come this soon.

I gave my approval with an easy mind because these days the entire nation shares the fate of having death on the doorstep.

His first words after the wedding: "She really has a beautiful figure." His clumsy chatter about his sweetheart made him popular at once.

Since leaving Kure he had been more diligent than ever. There was no one like him. Even during short breaks he never stopped tinkering with the equipment.

Did he fear that letting up might bring a moment's idleness and force him to face the reality of the situation?

A messenger boy calls delightedly: "Ensign Yoshida! For night rations tonight we're having bean soup and dumplings!"

He probably found that out from a sailor his own age in the galley. His elated smile exposes all his teeth.

Though side by side with older sailors, he is not mindful of their mental anguish; though under the command of squad chief Miyazawa, he is not acquainted with his agony.

Instead, he is wholly wrapped up in the thought of the special bean soup and dumplings, an overwhelming favorite among night rations; with much ado he spreads the word that we're to have it barely ten hours from now.

The plans call for us to charge into the enemy's midst at midnight tonight. If the hour for night rations finds us still okay, then the success of the operation will be beyond doubt.

Beyond doubt, too: our deaths in the ensuing battle.

That soup and dumplings—how will it taste?

Thinking to drop in on medical officer Lieutenant Commander Ishizuka, I go to the emergency medical station at the very top of the bridge. His pale face bent over, he is deep in a technical book.

"How are you, sir?" I ask. Silently, he nods.

A poet rather than a doctor, a man of letters rather than a soldier. He likes to sit in a corner of the officers' wardroom, usually lost in thought. It is barely three months since he came on board *Yamato* attached to headquarters, but his genuineness has endeared him greatly to his fellows.

Immediately before he came on board, he got married in Yokosuka, then hurried to his new posting: this I learned in putting the records in order after returning from the mission. His bride was a girl of seventeen.

Later still, I was visited by his widow. She told me the following:

At the time of the mission, she had traveled to Kure at the suggestion of her husband and was staying at the home of an acquaintance. Several days before that day of the assault, on an afternoon of heavy rain, he had gone ashore to spend the few short hours until evening with her; they tended to fall silent—was it only her imagination?—and from time to time they looked long and hard into each other's eyes.

The minutes flew, and it came time for him to return to the ship.

When on parting she cajoled him, "Can't you stay ashore longer next time? We could go for a hike somewhere," he suddenly took off his wrist watch and wrapped it firmly around her wrist. Naturally she was agitated; when she put her own hand over his and looked up into his face, he said with a smile, "Until I come next time take care of this watch as you would of me." Without looking back, he walked quickly away. He must have known that the mission was not far off.

She was too young to understand. Trusting with a light heart in fate, she believed her husband's words and, carefree, simply awaited the day of his return.

But far more painful to her than her own naivete in accepting unthinkingly the watch her husband was bequeathing to her was the fact that on April 7, 1945, at 2:30, the exact moment of her husband's death in battle, she was laughing, enjoying herself.

As it happened, she had gotten together with a few friends at the house of an acquaintance; she went out into the garden, which has an unbroken view of Kure Harbor, and without giving the least thought to her husband, amused herself happily—she rues that fact, rues it, but finds no peace.

After that brief shore leave, Lieutenant Commander Ishizuka lost his next chance to go ashore because he was on duty; and his last chance, too. On the night before we sailed, he had to perform an emergency appendectomy and missed the last boat. That night, rare for him, he got drunk.

Their actual married life: the day of the wedding and the day after.

Before the mission we gave free rein to our imaginations, thinking, from comments of his overheard at odd moments, that she was not his wife but his girlfriend, pure and innocent as a flower.

Had we known, on the night of the final liberty, that he had summoned his new bride to Kure, we would certainly have forced him to switch his time on call and pushed him into the boat for shore.

On his own initiative he had given up that last chance.

What had he sought in his young bride of seventeen? A noble beauty such as one dreams of? The purest love, innocent of reality? Or the normal, natural, healthy instincts of a wife?

Even had I known all this then, what words of sympathy could I possibly have spoken to his pale forehead?

0945 hours on: I stand watch. Ah, who would have thought I would stand *Yamato*'s last watch?

The clouds lower steadily; the ceiling: 1,000 meters.

Wind velocity: over twenty knots. Sudden showers.

Keeping watch is so difficult, and the duties of the watch are so important!

I feel as if my cheeks are twitching. Is the tension so great?

Standing ramrod-straight on the compass platform in the middle of the bridge, I grasp the binoculars in my sweaty hands.

In front of me and on both sides of me are massed the mouths of the voice tubes to all parts of the ship; they look like a honeycomb. Many phone receivers hem my face in, and above them is the mouth of the large voice tube to the antiaircraft command post (the captain's post during battle).

I press down on the grating until the soles of my feet hurt.

I keep a sharp lookout for submarines.

Visibility is poor, down to below eight kilometers. With the binoculars it is virtually impossible to spot periscopes, so great danger accompanies such conditions.

We rely heavily on the operation of our surface radar; but by the standards of the Japanese navy the periscope must be at least one meter out of the water for three minutes for surface radar to pick it up. For actual combat that is far from adequate.

We reach the spot designated for changing course.

The distance between *Asashimo* and us is too great, and so, abandoning the idea of turning back and reintegrating her into the formation, we turn immediately onto compass course south-southwest.

The bows of the ships now point directly at the enemy.

Lunch. Battle rations.

Leaning against the bulkhead, I hold the plate in one hand, the rice ball in the other. An unsettled meal.

My last taste of rice? I'd like to think I can stay this calm and composed all day, but it's hard to be optimistic.

Even as I am being assailed with dark premonitions, I eat this highly polished rice, this ceremonial food prepared with care.

Indescribably delicious. My final treat.

I sip the hot tea that fills my cup to the brim. It warms my throat and penetrates to my stomach.

After the meal, peace and harmony reign, the captain at the center.

Such an atmosphere must be extremely rare even on a training cruise, indeed on a cruise of any kind.

"Radar officer!"—out of the blue someone calls me. When I raise my head, it is the captain.

"Yes, sir!" I remain at my watch post but move one step toward him.

"You stated that you're an only son, didn't you?"

"That's right, sir." Several days before the mission, almost as if he foresaw this encounter, he sent around to all hands a list of questions about our family situations. I filled it out in detail and handed it in. At the bottom I wrote: "I have no anxieties about the future."

"You wrote, 'I have no anxieties about the future.' Is that true?" That he should remember anything about a mere ensign!

"I have no worries, sir."

"None at all?" How should I respond: no again? yes? I am unable to reply.

When I look up, his face is crimson as if in anger, his lips pressed sternly together. But I see that for a fleeting moment his penetrating gaze is filled with sorrow.

The famous captain, whose bravery and skill are legend. His nickname is "Gorilla," and he has the respect and affection of all the officers and men.

One night shortly before the mission, as officer in charge of the last boat ashore (it reached the wharf at nine o'clock), I took the captain ashore; and three hours later, at midnight, I brought him back to the ship in the first boat to pick up those on shore leave.

At a time when enemy attacks were frequent, the captain could not be away from the ship for any length of time. So direct and broad-minded that he could relax and refresh himself in so short a time?—I was unable to suppress a smile at the thought.

They say that when he went out in peacetime, he always wore civilian attire, and that he had an endearing soft spot for beauty—if he saw a woman who took his eye, he would follow her to find out where she lived.

I detect a gleam of gentleness even in the glances of his keen and highspirited staff officers.

It is not simply owing to the sense of ease, the languor brought on by full stomachs.

It is a true sympathy they afford us who are going to our deaths within a few paces of them, a sympathy almost like that between blood relatives.

From the Amami-Ōshima lookout comes a wireless message: "250 carrier-based enemy planes headed due north; keep close watch."

1200 hours. We have just reached the halfway point.

The entire task force advances serenely.

The commander in chief looks to each side of him and smiles a broad smile: "We got through the morning all right, didn't we?"

These are his first words since the mission began, when he took his seat in the commander in chief's chair, in front and to the right on the bridge. The sequence of alerts, the choice of zigzag, the speed, the changes of course—he has left everything to the captain of *Yamato;* and he has merely nodded silently in response to the reports of his chief of staff.

From now on, until the ship capsizes, he will sit, arms folded, like a rock amid the smoke of the guns and the rain of bullets. All those around him will be killed or wounded, but he will move not at all.

Was he too proud to assert control over this operation forced through over his opposition, opposition so strong he risked losing his command?

Or was this his silent protest against the fate of being remembered as the highest-ranking officer of an operation that will live in naval annals for its recklessness and stupidity?

A man of refreshing directness, the tall and graceful Admiral Itō.

The Battle Begins

1220 hours: our air search radar picks up three blips, each apparently a large formation.

In his usual guttural voice Petty Officer Hasegawa, chief of the antiaircraft radar room, gives a running commentary on their range and bearing. "Contacts. Three large formations. Approaching."

On the instant we send out emergency signals to every ship in the task force.

Each ship increases its speed to twenty-five knots. As one, they turn. "100 degrees exact." (Without changing its shape, the formation turns simultaneously onto a course of 100 degrees.)

Once the P.A. passes on word of the approaching planes, the ship, quiet already, becomes quieter still.

As the radar tracks the blips, the data is transmitted to us moment by moment over the voice tube: ". . . range

30,000 meters, bearing 160 degrees . . . second raid, range 25,000 meters, bearing 85 degrees. . . ."

How many times, in target practice, have we conducted such tracking? I am possessed by the illusion that we have already experienced searches under the same conditions, with the same battle positions, even with the same mood.

What is going on before my very eyes, indisputably, is actual combat—but how can I possibly convince myself of that fact?

The blips are not an imagined enemy but an enemy poised for the kill. The location: not our training waters, but hostile waters.

Nevertheless, as I pass the reports along mechanically, I am nonchalant, proceed too much by routine.

A battle against aircraft—it is at hand!

All the lookouts focus on the bearings of the approaching raids.

At this moment a light rain shrouds the ocean like a mist; visibility is now at its worst.

The moment we spot the American planes will probably be the moment they attack.

1232 hours: the gruff voice of the second watch—"Two Grummans, port 25 degrees, elevation 8 degrees, range 4,000 meters. Moving right."

Quickly I spot them with naked eye. The ceiling is between 1,000 and 1,500 meters.

We have spotted them, but conditions are the worst possible: they are already too close; aiming is very difficult.

"First raid: five planes . . . more than ten planes . . . more than thirty . . ."

A large squadron appears out of a gap in the clouds. Every ten or twelve planes peel off in formation and make a sweeping turn to starboard.

Dead ahead, another large flight. Already entering attack formation.

"More than one hundred enemy planes attacking!" Is it the navigation officer who calls this out?

Inevitable that both torpedoes and bombs will focus on *Yamato*.

The captain orders: "Commence firing."

Twenty-four antiaircraft guns and 120 machine guns open fire at the same moment.

The main guns of the escort destroyers, too, flash in unison.

The battle begins.

Here and now we fire the first shots of this desperate, death-inviting battle.

My baptism by fire. I feel like puffing out my chest, and my legs want to dance; restraining myself, I measure the weight pressing down on my knees.

As my whole body tingles with excitement, I observe my own exhilaration; as I grit my teeth, I break into a grin.

A sailor near me is felled by shrapnel. In the midst of the overwhelming noise, I distinguish the sound of his skull striking the bulkhead; amid the smell of gunpowder all around, I smell blood.

A shrill voice: "The enemy is using both torpedoes and bombs!"

On the left outer edge of the formation, *Hamakaze* all of a sudden seems to expose her crimson belly, then lifts her stern up into the air.

She sinks in a matter of only twenty or thirty seconds. She leaves behind only a sheet of white foam.

Of her crew, those who happen to be above decks fall into the water, blown off by the impact of the torpedoes and the blast of the exploding ship.

I understand that a good several dozen survivors drifted about for five hours on the periphery of the desperate air battle.

According to the story afterward of *Hamakaze's* senior officer (equivalent to executive officer), what led to her sinking was a slight hitch in taking evasive action.

Destroyers under attack use their agility and slender beam to evade torpedoes and bombs spotted with the naked eye. The captain sits atop the forward conn and is responsible for the front half of the ship; the senior officer sits atop the aft deckhouse, responsible for the stern half; in close coordination the two spot each torpedo and bomb coming toward them and, tracking them with the naked eye, take evasive action. Close cooperation between these two commanders and in particular the skill and decisiveness of the captain are the keys to survival.

On this day, when the first American squadron swooped down out of the clouds, something suffocating, overpowering filled *Hamakaze*. Such a thing had never happened before to *Hamakaze,* which had fought widely in southern waters.

Just as the first torpedo came at the ship from astern, throwing up a pillar of spray as it hit the water, in that instant, for less than a second, the senior officer was transfixed by it and simply watched it come; and perhaps because he was slow to inform the captain and the ship could dodge only a bit, the torpedo hit her in the stern and blew away the rudder.

In almost no time thereafter bombs landed one after another on the disabled ship. She was enveloped in columns of water, pillars of fire.

The tracks of the torpedoes are a beautiful white against the water, as if someone were drawing a needle through the water; they come pressing in, aimed at *Yamato* from a dozen different directions and intersecting silently.

Estimating by sight their distance and angle on the plotting board, we shift course to run parallel to the torpedoes and barely succeed in dodging them.

We deal first with the closest, most urgent one; when we get to a point far enough away from it that we can be sure we have dodged it, we turn to the next. Dealing with them calls for vigilance, calculation, and decision.

The captain is out in the open in the antiaircraft command post overlooking the whole ship. Two ensigns attend him and plot on the maneuver board the torpedoes coming from all directions, indicating them to him with pointers.

The navigation officer sits in the captain's seat on the bridge; acting as one, the two men operate the ship.

Coming over the voice tube, the captain's orders deafen me. His is a terrible and angry voice, biting off the ends of words.

Bombs, bullets focus on the bridge.

Opening her engines with their 150,000 horsepower to full throttle, straining at her top battle speed of twenty-seven knots, and turning her rudders hard to either side, *Yamato* continues her desperate evasive maneuvers.

This ship boasts of being as stable on open sea as on terra firma; even so she experiences extreme listing and vibration. The creaking of her hull and the grating of her fittings make a din.

Before we know it, we have dodged several torpedoes; at last we take one hit on the port bow.

The first wave of enemy attackers flies off.

There is virtually no list, but bombs have made two direct hits near the aft tower.

The American planes are in the main Grumman F6Fs (fighter planes), TBFs (torpedo bombers), and Curtiss SB2Cs (bombers). Most of their bombs are probably 25s (250 kilo bombs).

The tracks of the torpedoes are obvious and easy to spot, but aren't they somewhat faster than the torpedoes we've seen before? Thus the navigation officer.

He looks to both sides and says with a smile: "One torpedo finally got us, didn't it." No one responds.

A very skillful attack. To judge by their dexterity in dodging our antiaircraft fire and their fearlessness in taking aim, these must be the elite of the American forces. Thus the chief of staff.

The admiral, face kindly as always, sits with arms folded, absolutely motionless.

The chief of staff, all smiles, praises the enemy rather cheerfully.

Litter bearers carry three bodies almost stealthily from the bridge. Bullets must have gotten them.

Stealing glances at that scene and ashamed and angry because of my poor form in doing so, I feel as well a touch of self-pity.

Things return to a momentary tranquillity. The mood of friendly chatter is very similar to what we feel on completing a drill.

The Radar Compartment Takes a Bomb

A messenger from the chief of the fire control division, in a high-pitched voice: "The aft radar compartment appears to have taken a hit. Investigate the damage and report immediately."

The aft radar compartment (the antiaircraft director). It is one of my posts; had I not happened to be on deck watch, I might have been on duty there.

Lieutenant (jg.) Ōmori (chief radar officer), whom I have just relieved on watch, apparently headed straight there.

The boyish face of Lieutenant Ōmori, the bittersweet smile of Petty Officer Hasegawa, chief of the radar compartment, and the faces of many of their subordinates appear before my mind's eye as I run to the ladder at the aft side of the bridge and start down. To the right of the rail, as if eating into the iron bulkhead, a chunk of flesh. I brush it off with my elbow, and it goes sliding away.

"Hey, Radar! Outside you'll never make it for the bullets. Take the inside route!" It is a junior signal officer calling from atop the flag deck. His sharp voice cuts through the rain of bullets and strikes my ear.

He is kind enough to worry lest I throw my life away. Even as busy as he is.

Thanks. I turn my head and with my hand signal "Roger." But there is no time to do as he advises.

Climbing down through the inside of the bridge would be safer, but it takes time to open the doors dogged down for battle. That wouldn't suit this emergency.

It's my duty. And many shipmates have died already in my stead.

Sliding down the upright ladder, twenty meters tall, in a flash, I run. The smell of gunpowder assails my nose.

I have scraped the palms of my hands badly on the sides of the ladder, and the skinned places burn painfully.

An officer who stands exposed from the chest up in a side machine gun turret happens to look around. Our eyes meet as I run.

Ensign Takada, my classmate.

With his iron helmet down over his eyes, his swarthy face smiling, he calls in his Osaka dialect, "Take care, now," and waves his pointer.

Answering promptly, "Wilco," I run past without a glance. Who would have thought that this was to be my last sight of you, you son of a good Osaka family, you!

As I am about to rush past bomb damage at the base of the funnel, I meet Ensign Sukeda of the same division. Blood drips from two spots on his white headband; leaning on a cane, he can barely walk.

His post is the aft secondary fire control command post. It took a direct hit. No one doubted that all the men were killed; how did he escape death? Not giving in to his severe wounds, he must be on his way to make his report.

He is always affable and sweet-tempered, but he throws me only a brief sharp glance.

With rain gear in tatters and shoulders hunched, his slight figure seen from behind makes a pathetic sight. Perhaps because he has lost so much blood, he is so done in that I cannot bear to look at him.

When he has reported and lets up, he'll probably simply collapse.

Silently nodding to him, I hurry on.

I race to the area forward of the radar compartment. Not a trace of the ladder. I summon a deck hand and climb down a line.

The antiaircraft radar compartment, solid and safe. It was about three meters on a side and had steel bulkheads on all four sides, but the bomb has split it cleanly in two and blown away the upper half.

It is as if someone had taken an axe and split a bamboo tube. The bomb, a direct hit, must have sliced way in at an angle and then exploded.

Tuned and retuned in preparation for today's decisive battle, the instruments have been scattered in all directions. I don't recognize the debris. Not even any pieces left.

Just as I begin to think that everything must have been blown away, I notice a chunk of flesh smashed onto a panel of the broken bulkhead, a red barrel of flesh about as big around as two arms can reach.

It must be a torso from which all extremities—arms, legs, head—have been ripped off.

Noticing four hunks scattered nearby, I pick them up and set them in front of me.

To the charred flesh are stuck here and there pieces of khaki-colored material, apparently scraps of military uniform. The smell of fat is heavy in the air.

It goes without saying that I cannot tell where head and arms and legs might have been attached.

That it should be impossible to tell one corpse from another!

As I lift them, they are still hot from burning; when I run my hand over them, they feel like the bark of a rough tree.

My fellow officers and men who were alive and at work

here until a few minutes ago, and these hunks of flesh: one and the same, separated only by time!

How can I believe that?

The lives lodged in these four bodies—where have they gone?

The other eight men have been completely blown away; not even the stench of their deaths is left to float in the air.

What emptiness!

How did they die, those beings who only a moment ago were so real?

I cannot stop doubting, stop marveling.

It is not grief and resentment. It is not fear. It is total disbelief. As I touch these hunks of flesh, for a moment I am completely lost in thought.

A wave of sound comes smashing toward me from astern. My legs tremble ominously.

I look up into the attack of the second wave, coming in from the stern on the port side.

For shame. I have duties on the bridge. This isn't the place for me to die.

Already I feel the concussion from bombs exploding. Soon a cloud of bullets will engulf me.

Head down, with one hand touching the handrail, I make a mad dash. My eyes see nothing at all.

The ship is steaming at full speed, and wind stirred up by her forward motion surges along the whole passageway.

Just as I start to scramble up the ladder at the base of the main tower, my eyes go taut—perhaps because my whole body is so keyed up: no sign of that machine-gun mount, Ensign Takada's post.

Heartsick, I turn my head and stare with wide-open eyes: a great gouged-out spot, and clouds of white smoke boiling up out of it—that is all.

People, guns, mount—in one instant wiped out without a trace?

Ensign Takada. Forgive me.

A moment ago, you shouted encouragement to me through the rain of bullets, but I was caught up in the danger to my men and did not respond. I ran on past without even a word of reply.

That you have met such a cruel death—is it because I was remiss in encouraging you?

You who were a good man and true, so adept at keeping everyone else's glass full. You of the white teeth, who often broke into a loud laugh.

With eyes squeezed shut, I race up the ladder.

Had I passed that spot twenty or thirty seconds earlier, the blast of the direct hit would have enveloped me, and you and I would have died together.

I rush up the ladder, spurring on my daunted self, whipping up my hostility, repeating in a loud voice the report I must deliver to the division officer: "All crew dead; instruments completely destroyed; compartment unusable."

Even at its loudest, my voice is lost in the sounds of destruction, the din.

The shouting is necessary to spur myself on.

Bullets ping at my back; their blasts fan my waist.

I report immediately to the division officer.

The air search radar, a crucial weapon of our defense

against planes, has thus been destroyed at the start of the battle.

The enemy planes, pressing in on us out of a dark sky, we confront with only our unaided eyesight.

A low voice whispering deep in my ear is so faint it seems on the point of fading away.

The voice of Lieutenant Ōmori (senior radar officer), which came over the phone just before I took the watch three hours ago. His last words linger in my ear.

"You, Ensign Yoshida, I've given you nothing but difficult tasks, made you work . . . Sorry for that . . ."

Not so. It's I who was remiss.

"You . . . You . . .": the voice does not stop. It whispers, as if in reproach.

He's already fallen. Dead. How can I possibly respond?

Lieutenant Usubuchi (in charge of the aft secondary guns) is killed by a direct hit.

The young warrior who was both wise and courageous leaves behind not one bit of flesh, not one drop of blood.

He hoped by dying to awaken new life. His body, offered up in the cause of a genuine national rebirth, has disappeared into thin air.

The Fierce Assault: Second Wave

The second wave, too: more than one hundred planes. From the port beam. Mainly torpedo bombers?

Seeing that the covering fire of cruiser *Yahagi* is fierce

and accurate, one group of the attacking planes heads for her.

Twenty torpedo tracks head toward *Yamato*. We take three hits on the port side. In the neighborhood of the aft tower.

Part of the auxiliary rudder sustains damage.

The overwhelming number of torpedoes has made it impossible, even with this ship's agility, to dodge them all.

A veritable circle of fire closes in on us: from above, from all points of the compass, glistening.

The curtain of antiaircraft fire *Yamato* throws up is without parallel in our navy. With its carpet of explosions in brilliant red, purple, yellow, and green, it is not an insignificant menace; but its power to intimidate and destroy is far less than we had supposed.

Conceding from the outset that the sacrifice of some planes is inevitable, the American formation discards roundabout tactics to evade the curtain of bullets. Instead, it surges straight ahead, an avalanche, on the course best suited for taking aim.

Not only the fighter planes and bombers, attacking at a steep downward angle, but even the torpedo bombers, attacking at a gentle angle of descent, zigzag as soon as they have dropped their payloads and, evading our flak, carry out close-range strafing.

Moreover, discarding the ironclad rule that one attacks at a steep angle from a height of 3,000 meters, they adapt to conditions, shifting to shallower dives that make use of the heavy clouds: very original on their part.

In aiming torpedoes and bombs, one must hold to a given course for a certain distance. But the American planes reduce that vulnerable interval to the very minimum, switching quickly to close-quarter tactics, swooping about like swallows.

If, like Japanese planes, they would hold longer to a given course, during that time our targets would move only in a vertical plane. We could more easily aim and fire the antiaircraft guns. But targets that attack even while zigzagging to left and right necessitate sizable and swift corrections in aim both horizontally and vertically. Aiming at such a target is far too difficult for simple machine guns. Our percentage of hits is very low.

For each five rounds, the guns fire one tracer shell. By watching how the tracer's tea-colored trajectory intersects the target, the gunners ascertain their error and adjust for distance and angle. Still, when the angular velocity is so great, a hit is difficult even at very close range.

Vainly attempting to track the targets, the gunners wind up at best close on the tails of the attacking planes.

Given their great flying skill and accuracy of aim, it is natural for American pilots to attack this way. But it is also comparatively easy for them to advance upon us from out of the clouds: the ceiling is low, the curtain of fire from the main batteries is thin and restricted to the horizontal plane, and the antiaircraft guns are silenced.

Moreover, we cannot hide the fact that our machine gunners are dazed by the overwhelming number of enemy planes and by their repeated attacks.

It stands to reason. The muzzle velocity of a 25 mm machine-gun bullet is less than 1,000 meters per second, barely five or six times the average speed of the American planes.

Using tracers to correct the aim of weapons at such a

disadvantage for speed is like chasing after butterflies with our bare hands.

For our air defense training we have used streamers or balloons as targets, and we have rejoiced or despaired according to our performance against targets able only to float.

To the eyes of machine gunners trained in this fashion, an American plane soaring through the sky is a marvel, an apparition.

The gunners are the focus of an unremitting deluge of explosions, relentless light, sound, and concussion.

Crushing defeats at the hands of attacking airplanes have occurred recently with great frequency. The lessons survivors draw all point to this issue of technology and urge vehemently that some kind of drastic countermeasure is imperative.

Yet the gunnery school normally reacts to these arguments with the assertion that "the low ratio of hits is attributable to the poor ability of the gunners and to the inadequacy of their training." That response offers nothing positive.

It was just about a month before the mission that someone discovered, alongside such an observation in a training manual circulated by the gunnery school, in large bold letters: "This is utter nonsense. Lieutenant Usubuchi."

In addition, he had pasted beside the passage a slip of paper on which he had written: "The inadequacy lies not in training but in zeal and ability for scientific research." It continued in the following vein:

"Don't you know about the latest English antiaircraft guns, which have neutralized the cross-channel bombing of the Germans? They attach chains several hundred meters long to high-angle artillery shells, add a weight, and fire them with rockets at a speed not less than that of bullets. The chain describes a circle twice its own length for a diameter and sweeps toward the enemy planes. It's an easy matter to achieve a kill ratio of at least 50 percent. There is a world of difference between the concept (employed in all Japanese antiaircraft fire) of using a point to hit a point, and the idea of using a geometric plane to catch a point. Given this state of affairs, it's meaningless to talk of inadequacies of training."

It goes without saying that all the junior officers signed their names beneath that statement.

Even this excess drew no reprimand, no punishment from anyone. That part of the training manual was circulated among the staff officers in absolute silence; that was all.

The disparaging comment—"The world's three great follies, prize examples of uselessness, are the Great Wall of China, the pyramids, and *Yamato*"—evokes abusive words, shouted through the ship—"The only way to save the navy is to execute all officers of the rank of lieutenant commander up!" And still no compunction.

Bombs rain down squarely on the turrets, each equipped with three 25 mm machine guns (the turrets are about three meters by three meters by three meters). One after another the turrets fly up into the air.

The highest rises twenty meters, turns over several times, and then falls back down with a crash.

A scene of carnage with no place for the living.

Casualties among the machine gunners are staggering.

Moreover, because bombs have severed the wires, power

outages follow in rapid succession; desperate repair work is of no avail; electric-powered weapons turn one after the other into useless chunks of steel.

Firing the guns reverts necessarily to a matter of sighting down the barrel.

Director turrets stand somewhat above the three or four machine-gun turrets they govern. The direction and angle of the director turret are transmitted electrically to each of the subordinate turrets; normally the only task at the guns themselves is to pull the trigger. But with the power disrupted and the automatic aiming system inoperative, there is nothing for it but to aim each gun independently.

Our aim becomes even more inaccurate. We shrink back, become unsettled: the signs are clear.

White smoke rises from the vicinity of the aft flight deck.

Very near misses land to port and starboard and in the water ahead. Time and again we plunge ahead into a forest of geysers.

Water, ten times more than a torrential shower, cascades in, almost shattering the ports of the bridge.

Chaos everywhere from the wild force of the water.

The chart stand, awash in filthy water, is a terrible sight. Wiping it off, I swallow bitter tears.

Water runs down my neck to my chest, to my waist; though lukewarm, it gives me goosebumps when it soaks into my underwear.

The chinstrap of my helmet, biting into my jaw, is cold.

Unrelenting Fierce Assault

As soon as the second wave departs, the third wave attacks, right on its heels.

From the port beam 120 or 130 planes, sweeping in like a sudden rainshower.

Several bombs score direct hits near the funnel.

Lieutenant (jg.) Tsukagoshi, Lieutenant (jg.) Igaku, Ensign Sekihara, Ensign Shichiri fall in battle, one after the other.

Report after report comes in that officers in charge of machine guns have been killed.

All the bombs aimed at the bridge have missed their mark but have hit the machine guns surrounding and protecting the bridge.

Torpedo hits, two of them, on the port side.

The needle of the inclinometer just barely begins to move.

Because of the consecutive torpedo hits, many among the damage-control crews are dead or wounded. It becomes difficult to perform the tasks involved in controlling the flooding.

When a torpedo strikes, water pours into one part of a flood control sector. These sectors are small compartments—the whole ship is divided up into 1,150 of them—designed to restrict the area of flooding. But the pressure of the water gradually builds up against the metal bulkheads that form the barrier between flooded and unflooded compartments. The water finally bursts through those bulkheads, and the flooding spreads.

The bulkheads must be reinforced from the unflooded

side with great wooden braces to prevent their breaking—this is the task of the damage-control crews.

But new torpedo hits, continuing without letup, lend added impetus to the force of the rushing water, which destroys everything in its path. The damage-control crews have their hands full simply rescuing the men.

While they are at work on damage control, torpedoes strike one after the other, and in an instant sea water pours in and drives them to escape up the ladders to higher places. As they scramble up the cylindrical metal companionways, those higher up must be quick to throw the dogs, sealing the hatches beneath their feet and thus shutting off the water. Doing so secures a fall-back line.

To stomp on the head of the shipmate scrambling up the companionway after you and seal the hatch. To estimate how fast the water is rising and size up the situation in an instant.

How intensely difficult to do! An impossible task: even the fiercest training is of no avail.

Through hatches heedlessly left open for the sailors racing up the companionways, the avalanche of water rushes on.

Thus the list increases faster than expected.

Already my whole body feels uneasy.

If the list progresses to five degrees, it will impede the conveyance of artillery shells and will cut our battle strength by half.

Moreover, the sense of having lost our equilibrium is critical to morale. We cannot afford to wait.

Correct the list now by balancing port and starboard, flooding the starboard compartments, the exact counterparts of the flooded compartments on the port side: there is no alternative.

The order is given to let in 3,000 tons of water.

Inevitably, the flooding will make us ride lower in the water—and sharply decrease our speed; but the step is unavoidable.

The flooding is engineered by the flooding control station. Lamps flash automatically on the control board to indicate flooded areas; when the buttons for the same areas on the opposite side of the ship are pushed, valves open to let sea water in. This capability, central to *Yamato's* ability to defend herself and much boasted of—is it too only a passing hope?

"Aft water-control headquarters has taken one torpedo hit, one direct bomb hit." A report transmitted via voice tube.

The staff officers on the bridge are mute, speechless.

Heaven isn't on our side?

This all-important control center, located in the bowels of the stern because it is so vulnerable to repeated hits of bombs and torpedoes.

The assault has been marked by tenacity, as if the attackers well knew its location and aimed at it.

The destruction of the flooding control station makes it impossible to flood the starboard compartments.

The worst possible situation, not foreseen even in our training. That it should become the single overriding reality!

Come to think of it, in training we repeated drills that were impractical, too easy.

The American forces seem to be concentrating their entire strength on two tactics: continuous assault, and torpedoes aimed at one side.

The captain calls several times: "Be quick about restoring the trim!" His orders are transmitted to the necessary posts via the voice tubes.

But the list is not easy to correct. There is no alternative. We must flood starboard compartments that are not part of the flood-control system.

The enemy, attacking at our feet, is bent on capsizing us. Danger. No matter what the sacrifice, it must be made.

It is decided that the best course is to flood the engine and boiler rooms. These two rooms are the largest and lowest compartments equipped with water pumps, which make it possible to flood them rapidly; a marked effect on the list can be expected.

The damage control officer (the executive officer holds this post concurrently) decides to flood them immediately.

The engine room and the boiler room, operating at full tilt—the posts of the black gang.

Until this moment these men have made the ship go, battling sweltering heat and deafening noise, uncomplaining throughout. Confined in the depths of the ship with no way of knowing how the battle is going, their bodies bathed in sweat and oil, they can converse and communicate only by hand signals.

Naturally enough, the emergency crews controlling the pumps hesitate.

"Hurry!" I urge the control room on with a phone call.

The abandon-ship buzzer sounded to both those rooms: is it too late, too?

In the instant the water rushes in, the black gang on duty are dashed into pieces, turned into drops of spray.

In that instant they see nothing and hear nothing; shattered into lumps, they dissolve; turned into swirls of water, they disappear.

How ferocious the pressure of the seething water!

At the price of several hundred lives, we barely restore the ship's trim.

Even so, how pathetic to be reduced to half our power! The needle on the speedometer falls back as if broken.

On one leg and limping, we fight off the encircling swallows.

A Sudden Turn for the Worse

The fourth wave comes flying at us from the port bow. More than 150 planes.

Several torpedoes gouge sections out of the port side.

Many bombs score direct hits on aft tower, aft deck.

The attack on the bridge becomes ever fiercer.

After the planes release their bombs and turn from side to side, they press in directly at the bridge with all guns blazing.

Pillars of fire. A droning sound. Gunpowder smoke blowing in through the port, their breath, as it were.

The flushed faces of the American pilots bear in on us one after the other. I have the illusion that they are reproaching me to my face.

Their eyes are either opened wide or else shut so tightly that their faces contort. Most have their mouths open and almost ecstatic expressions on their faces.

If struck by our guns, their planes spout fire for a moment and plunge into the ocean; but even then they have already dropped their torpedoes and bombs.

In the entire battle not a single pilot is so rash as to crash his plane into us.

Coming in again and again on the ideal approach, precisely, exactly, calmly, they evoke in us a sense of exhilaration. Virtuosi. Theirs is a strength we cannot divine, a force we cannot fathom.

At the moment all we can do is keep the damage to a minimum, conserve our fighting strength, and wait for the enemy to dissipate his numerical advantage.

But is there any chance at all of that?

The narrow lookout ports on the bridge are eye-high, scooped out horizontally and extending all the way around.

Most of the bullets that come flying at these windows bounce off and, with a puff of smoke, fall away in all directions. They seem to dance playfully.

There is no way to gauge where the explosions will be or in which direction the bullets are going.

How can we avoid being hit?

We are utterly naked before them.

Most of the men on the bridge, without thinking, have thrown themselves flat on the deck and are looking up at the American planes coming in.

There is even more danger in looking straight into the barrels of their guns; but it is too unsettling to be shot at by someone we can't see. We are driven by the impulse at least to catch sight of our sworn enemies.

In our midst, the commander in chief, who as before does not stir.

The chief navigation officer, standing erect.

In front of them, leaning halfway out the port and watching for torpedoes, the indomitable Lieutenant (jg.) Yamamori, graduate of the naval academy.

Heroic action of the sort he always boasted about?

Suddenly a heavy weight falls on me from three directions—front, rear, and left side. The sailors in front of me and behind me and the officer on my left, all within elbow-rubbing distance, have been struck down simultaneously.

Breaking loose, I free myself from the weight of their bodies. The three bodies, leaning on one another, twist and fall.

The two sailors look like clothing that has been shucked off. Instantaneous death.

Ensign Nishio, who had been on my left, abruptly gets to his feet as I watch him, then falls on his left knee, his lips already losing their color. Trying to bind up his right thigh?

Gushing blood swells the towel and turns it bright red. In almost no time, the color drains from his face.

A fairly deep wound—I immediately summon corpsmen. They spread a stretcher, and Ensign Nishio lies face down on it, then lifts his head. A faint smile appears on his face, as if he is looking up at something, and he loses consciousness.

The peace that comes from having nothing to regret? or a farewell to someone?

He of the handsome face: the sublime look on his dying face is so vivid that for some time his smile does not fade from my eyes.

He keeps a photograph on his person at all times. Only a few close friends have gotten a look at it; they all say it is of a good-looking woman "pure, with a touch of melancholy about her."

It goes without saying that, along with Ensign Mori, he was an object of envy, the two of them considered the luckiest persons in the world.

Moreover, the fact that he put up with the words of banter and envy, wearing a smile and proudly silent throughout, made them tease him all the more.

The thought of her no doubt warmed his heart even as his body grew cold on the stretcher.

After returning alive, I learn the truth by chance from his service record and from the bundle of letters at headquarters from her who waited so eagerly for his return.

She was his younger sister. Their parents were dead, and there were no other brothers or sisters. The two of them were alone in the world. The one for whom he had an abiding love, whose picture he would never let out of his grasp, was none other than his own flesh and blood.

Those three bodies, of Ensign Nishio and the two sailors, saved me by shielding me from flying shrapnel. We were less than a foot apart.

My uniform is red in several places, dyed with spatters of blood.

Radar messenger Leading Seaman Kishimoto, seventeen years old: his lips are quivering. Terror-stricken at the chunks of flesh? the gore all around him?

What is more, the reports he himself transmits brim with the ferocity of the battle and the misfortunes of his shipmates.

I look him straight in the eye and give him one blow on the cheek. His boyish face reddens; the quivering ceases. A sweet fellow.

Enemy planes fly in at us, then veer out of sight, time and again; casualties on the bridge gradually mount.

Even though we have cleared away the lumps of flesh that were scattered all over, the bloodstains remain, like birthmarks.

Already more than half those on the bridge are dead; it is nice to have much more room to move around in, but there is no time to stop and think about who has died.

Most of those still standing firm here have towels and bandages wrapped around arms, legs, heads. A hard fight.

I go to the upper radar compartment. The faces of some of the members of that surface radar crew have suddenly appeared to my mind's eye.

Dislodged by the vibration, the radar equipment has become wholly unusable. Is it that the concussion from our own guns, the continuous damage, is unprecedented?

That things have come to such a pass! One can't help concluding that the instruments were poorly installed.

This equipment, judged most reliable by the fleet radarmen, performs in the end not at all.

In the narrow compartment, the sailors are piled together; linking arms and legs, they endure the shaking and the shuddering. These are the radarmen, pride of the Japanese navy.

Shrapnel from machine-gun bullets bursts at them through the bulkhead, but not one of them budges.

Sending off sparks, a piece of shrapnel zings through the compartment and, as smoke billows up, grazes the neck of Leading Seaman Mori before falling to the deck. Under his ear a fat red blister forms.

Leading Seaman Mori, obedient and able radarman. He picks up the piece of shrapnel and, head still bent, holds it out to me; it is the size of the end of my thumb, torn and sharp. It is pleasantly warm in my palm.

Touching his neck, he crinkles his eyes and smiles.

From that point on until the ship sinks, I have no chance to descend to this spot again to urge them to escape.

Ah, what were they waiting for at that moment, silent, their bodies tangled and prostrate? what were they preparing for?

Still in that posture, they shared the fate of the ship.

Some of them had wives and children. Many others were young men with ruddy faces.

Leading Seaman Aoyama was the sole survivor; according to him, thereafter, just before the ship sank, they collapsed in a heap amid the roar of explosions and repeated concussions. The shadow of death hung over them all.

Wanting to escape, he called out, "Let's go!" No response. A few men merely looked up. Even though he struck them on the shoulder and kicked them, they simply collapsed.

Such behavior occurs quite often among men who have no specific tasks to perform during a battle.

The clock ticks away as they wait and endure, beleaguered by concussion, power failure, sudden turns, and bombs; what is more, they have no idea what the situation is and are oppressed by a sense of doom: "Is this the moment I die? Is this?" It's not something the ordinary person can endure.

First the tip of one's tongue goes numb, then one's hands and feet; one loses the ability to move; finally the pupils of one's eyes open wide. The body is still warm, but in fact one is dead, a corpse.

Then it is simply a matter of waiting anxiously for the body to die.

Yet weren't these the most dedicated sailors of all? And even they had to give in to the god of death.

The communications compartment boasted of its complete impregnability against water. But torpedoes converge on it. It too succumbs to flooding.

Here we lose over half the communications personnel, including the communications officer.

Yamato, flagship of the task force, has no radio capability.

We're down now to signal lights and signal flags.

Take away ears and mouth, and even a giant can do little.

Radio officer Ensign Nakatani must have died too, at his post intercepting enemy communications. Because he was a *nisei,* his conduct always attracted attention; I can guess that his death was as splendid as the deaths of his fellows.

According to the testimony of Ensign Watanabe, who was the only communications division officer to survive, the work of intercepting and translating enemy communications went on serenely and surely right up to the moment the communications compartment flooded.

Afterward, when the end of the war brought with it the restoration of communications, I reported these facts to his mother, far away in that foreign land. She wrote me in reply:

"There is nothing that gives me greater joy than to know that Kunio fought until the very end, exerting himself to his utmost at his post, and that he attained a death of which, as a Japanese, he need not be ashamed. When I heard that Kunio had died in battle, I was overcome with grief for three months; but learning how Kunio died, I have taken heart. Our whole family reveres his memory."

The needle of the clinometer swings from fifteen degrees to seventeen. Actual speed: twelve knots, perhaps thirteen.

In the rush to restore trim, we flood other compartments on the starboard side in addition to the engine and boiler rooms; but because we cannot make use of the outermost compartments, this step has minimal effect.

Concentrated bombing wipes out the second damage control station, nucleus of our defenses. All the officers at the station are killed, including the administrative officer.

The executive officer, whose normal station it is (he is concurrently the damage control officer), happened to be in the first damage control station and is unharmed.

That blow cuts to pieces our ability to defend ourselves. The ship is unable to put up any concerted fight.

Restoring trim has become virtually impossible.

The Bitter Struggles of Our Escort Ships

While we are thus engaged, the fifth wave attacks suddenly from ahead. More than one hundred planes.

At this moment *Yahagi* (light cruiser) lies dead in the water 3,000 meters ahead of us and is attempting to get *Isokaze* to come alongside.

The commander of the Second Destroyer Squadron is in *Yahagi*. In this last moment before she sinks, is he trying to abandon *Yahagi* and transfer to lightly damaged *Isokaze?*

A commanding officer's death in battle is an enormous obstacle to the conduct of an operation; it will probably contribute to demoralization.

Still, in a hopeless situation like this and, what is more, in a special-attack operation that will end inevitably in death, so undisguised a measure by one commander to prolong his life leaves me with a strange feeling. He must be acting on his own initiative.

It was only natural that after returning alive from the operation he became a target of criticism. The young officers were particularly sharp in their attacks.

Under these conditions, some of the American planes about to attack us veer off and head for the two ships.

Yahagi takes several torpedoes and sinks, sending up only a dark spray.

Isokaze too lies dead in the water and is belching black smoke.

Even though she narrowly escapes sinking, she appears to have taken several direct bomb hits.

Fuyutsuki to starboard and *Yukikaze* to port, dashing along and breaking through curtains of water several times taller than they, signal us in *Yamato:* "Everything in order."

The two stalwart ships fighting gamely, staking their all.

Think of it! The fighting spirit and the readiness of the two ships, down to the last sailor.

Of the nine ships assigned to protect us, these two are the only ones doing their job.

The others are either lying on the bottom or listing from their wounds.

These two ships, still capable of high speed, all that is left of the elite task force: will they, too, meet cruel defeat?

No word at all from *Asashimo,* straggling far behind.

Surrounded by American planes and fighting desperately against heavy odds, *Asashimo* has probably already met her fate.

Afterward we learned there was not a single survivor.

No matter how violent and instantaneous the sinking, there are always at least a few survivors: those fortunate ones who happen to be posted above decks are sent flying and wind up floating in the water.

I understand that communications ended a few minutes after the battle began with the final message: "Engaging thirty enemy planes."

The few who escaped death at the hands of the bombs. As they drifted about in the water, despairing because no consort ships came into view, to say nothing of islands, their strength must finally have given out.

A Brief Respite

No planes overhead. The enemy is taking a brief respite.

It is the first lull since the second wave.

Truly countless bombs have hit *Yamato,* of course, and the situation is already quite unclear. Shipboard communications have been totally disrupted.

The chain of command is not functioning normally. Even the voice tubes, which take the place of the telephones, have been severely damaged. All we can rely on is the messengers.

Find an uninjured sailor, slap him on the shoulder, and have him run a message. But as soon as he goes to slide down the ladder, even before he is out of sight, he is hit by machine gun bullets and falls.

This giant body is left to total disintegration; its parts, lacking connection with each other, head separately on the path to destruction.

In the vicinity of the aft deck, silhouettes of men who struggle to fight fires. Their movements gradually become sluggish.

Many of the machine-gun turrets are completely destroyed, making the deck a desolation, leaving only pitted lumps of steel.

A chunk of human flesh, thin but the size of a man, hangs down from high atop an arm of the rangefinder and sways unceasingly.

Where did it come flying from? That's ten meters above the deck.

The weather deck, painted jet black but now thoroughly chewed up, has changed color.

The exposed instruments are all damaged. The wires strung like a spider's web between the main tower and the aft tower are gone without a trace.

In days gone by this giant brimmed with a unique feeling of power. The machine-gun turrets and antiaircraft guns, stacked impressively one atop the other like well-developed biceps. The strong line of the deck, bending in a bit toward the bow, slicing into the waves. But now she is only a shadow of her former self.

She floats in the water like a chunk of waterlogged wood, light brown.

Because of the excessive list, the shells of middle size and above cannot be moved. The carts carrying the shells would tip over; it is still more dangerous to carry them by hand.

The antiaircraft guns and the secondary guns are completely silent. Only the machine guns remain for the last desperate battle.

I understand that many bombs have hit lower down on the bridge, that all medical personnel at the emergency sick bay have been killed.

The swarm of wounded men, and in their midst the medical corpsmen urgently wielding their scalpels: a bomb blast mows them all down. A scene of carnage, encompassing the death of Lieutenant Commander Ishizuka, who leaves behind his innocent bride.

There is no way for the innumerable other casualties to be reported, nor is there even anyone who knows how they died.

Already many reports of the battle deaths of officers have piled up; in time they stop coming, and so pass out of my mind.

Countless bullets have poured in on the bridge. The attrition among the men is severe.

A bomb falls at us from straight ahead, grows in almost no time—a black dot, a pebble, a spindle. Just as I hold my breath thinking it will land right on top of us, it whizzes past, barely missing our heads, and falls away.

And yet of the staff officers stationed on the bridge, in the antiaircraft command post, in the firing tower, and in the fire control director, not one has fallen. It has to be divine aid.

What does this luck bring in its train?

How much time has elapsed since the first shot was fired? Hasn't it been only an instant?

At least for me, the aftertaste is like that from a stint of good hard work or several minutes of pleasure.

A sense of delight bubbles secretly in my breast. I am not the slightest bit tired.

Remembering my empty stomach, I eat some candy as I keep my eye on the clinometer.

The sweets and cookies I had stuffed into both pockets of my raingear are already half gone. Have I fumbled for them before without realizing?

Delicious. Indescribably delicious.

The Rush to the Kill

The sixth, seventh, and eighth waves of the attack come one after the other. Each about 100 planes. From the port side and from astern.

A hunch sends shivers up my spine: is the enemy taking advantage of our loss of speed and trying to damage the rudder?

We are covered all over with wounds. What is more, we are down to half our power. Helpless.

Forming beautiful patterns, the torpedo tracks chase after our giant stern.

I turn my back to the stern, wringing my sweaty hands, and wait for the impact with senses honed.

The torpedoes hit aft. Floating in the air for a moment, the stern is mantled in pillars of flame, pillars of water.

Although damage to both rudders, main and auxiliary, is slight, the auxiliary-rudder steering room falls victim to flooding.

The auxiliary rudder is stuck hard to port; so even with the main rudder to starboard, the ship can make turns only to port. One side of our body is paralyzed.

Moreover, the steering room for the main rudder is also on the point of being flooded.

These are probably the tactics of the American forces:

Break through our curtain of fire by overwhelming it with sheer numbers of planes. Taking advantage of weather conditions, bombard us with torpedoes and bombs dropped at angles both gentle and steep;

Focus the torpedoes on one side and cut our speed drastically by rapidly increasing our list;

Conduct sure-fire bombing against a slow-moving ship and destroy our antiaircraft fire;

Smash the rudder with torpedoes from the rear. Then, another concentrated attack with torpedoes, the *coup de grâce.*

This strategy, it must be said, is carefully considered and resolute.

The navigation officer: "Step by step we can guess what the enemy will do. We think, 'He'll hit the rudder,' and he hits it. And there's nothing we can do about it. It's the height of absurdity."

The chief of staff: "Beautifully done, isn't it! When all is said and done, actual combat is the best training. In the early part of the war, we developed our skills while steadily on the advance. But in the latter part of the war, we have been simply retreating, and the enemy has caught up with us.

"At the beginning of the war we flung a challenge to

the world: how to attack capital ships with carrier planes. Now we get a brilliant answer thrust upon us."

Is this giant ship now on the point of losing her ability to maneuver?

Bombs, rocket shells, incendiary bombs pour down on the length and breadth of the ship, innumerable.

From the vicinity of the funnel, dense black smoke rises up. A fire below decks? That such a thing can happen even to this ship, which boasts of perfect defenses against fire!

A sudden increase in the list. Speed down to seven knots. We make a slight turn to port.

From our starboard bow *Kasumi* steams blindly at us, flying signal flags: "Have lost steering control." Torpedoes must have gotten its rudder.

Kasumi lists drunkenly.

How can we avoid a collision?

Exasperated by our own paralysis, we struggle and finally manage to dodge *Kasumi*.

For the first time since the battle began, laughter is heard on the bridge. Are we laughing at ourselves?

Phone calls from the steering compartment for the main rudder become more frequent. The officer in charge (a lieutenant junior grade) reports that the flooding has progressed to the compartment next to him.

Meanwhile, he calmly recites the position of the rudder moment by moment.

Suddenly he shouts twice, his voice understandably constricted: "Flooding imminent! Flooding imminent!"

Then, a moment's sounds of destruction, and communications break off completely.

On *Yamato*'s main tower the signal flag goes up: "Rudder damaged." This is the first time that flag has waved over this ship. It will also be the last time.

Writhing in agony on the surface of the water, this unsinkable giant ship is now an ideal target for bombs, nothing more.

Death Agonies

List: 35 degrees.

Is the main body of American planes gathering in the clouds and biding its time? Dividing up into small formations of a few planes or ten or a dozen planes, they rush in for the kill.

Against so weak a target, the attack brings them gratifying results.

We are unable to take evasive action, so all the bombs hit their target; prostrate on the deck of the bridge, we endure the concussions.

The death-blow bombing is brutal, not a single bomb wasted. The precision is virtually surgical.

But in the next instant, in a fleeting moment of emptiness, the thought bubbles up inside me: they may be the enemy, but they are doing a splendid job.

I experience the elation of being taught by true professionals.

The captain himself repeats several times: "Don't lose heart!" How many men heard his voice?

The ship's loudspeakers and the voice tubes are as good as completely destroyed. We depend entirely on the oral transmission of hoarse-voiced messengers.

Those within range of the captain's voice straighten their shoulders a bit and unclench their jaws—that is all.

Enormous geysers rise on port and starboard sides amidships. I feel as if the deck has been swept out from under my feet.

The navigation officer, with a sharp, inquisitorial tone in his voice: "Captain, didn't you see that last torpedo?"

The captain, from the upper antiaircraft command post: "No, I didn't."

The navigation officer, repeating: "Didn't you see it?" The side of his face I can see stiffens and flushes.

Will this torpedo at last be the fatal wound? It delivers a hard blow equivalent at least to the blast of several airborne torpedoes.

Has a submarine caught us off guard, approached, and zeroed in on us?

Or, with our extreme list, with the armor plating along the hull now out of the water, have the torpedo bombers concentrated their torpedoes on the ship's exposed and vulnerable belly?

It has absolutely enormous power, this mysterious torpedo.

A fitting end, filled with mystery, for this giant ship.

The needle of the clinometer takes a marked leap.

Feeling a slight tiredness, I brace one elbow on the deck and rest. I feel light-hearted.

It is an ideal list for propping oneself up at an angle.

Taking deep breaths, I eat a mouthful of candy. What's enjoying this taste? My flesh and blood, or my long-neglected appetite?

Remembering, I drink some soda. It had been hidden

in an inside pocket of my rain gear. The bubbles tickle my throat.

Its sweet taste, lingering on my tongue.

Suddenly, from within, a voice:

"You, you on the brink of death. Embrace death; enjoy the anticipation of death.

"What does death look like? What does the touch of death feel like?

"You, what do you have to show for your life? If anything, out with it!

"Isn't there anything at all you can be proud of at this moment?"

Head in hands, writhing: "My life has been short. I'm too young . . .

"Let me alone. Let me go. Don't transfix me. Don't tear me apart.

"I know better than anyone else how miserable it is to die . . ."

How weak, this muttering!

The mood of the people around me does not change. Exchanging gloomy glances, each checks to see that the others are still alive.

There is only fatigue, as after violent activity, when the body, warm in all its parts, seems almost to melt.

The emptiness in their eyes. Is it total self-oblivion?

For a moment, utter prostration. A desolation, as in the aftermath of a gale.

I have done battle—that memory is firm and unclouded.

Around me, quiet.

The needle of the clinometer rises, slipping its way, as it were, into the midst of this tranquillity.

The Breakup of the Task Force

The executive officer to the captain: "There's no hope of trimming the list."

Defying the extraneous noise, the clear voice of the executive officer comes cleanly through the sturdy voice tube, specially installed, that connects bridge and emergency command post.

It is my duty to repeat the message in a loud voice for the entire bridge.

The impossibility of trimming the list—the certainty that we will sink—the collapse of the mission—death. The association of ideas leads instantaneously to this conclusion.

There is no panic. But two or three men are propped up on one elbow, and their shoulders shake, as if in a spasm.

Amid all this, men crawling to the chair of the commander in chief: the staff officers, aren't they? The final conference?

The loss of the flagship, especially this giant ship, forces a drastic change in tactics.

At last the commander in chief, abruptly raising himself up, stares out ahead at the water rising and falling at a skewed angle.

On reflecting afterward, I realize that in that moment the admiral had reached the direct and resolute conclusion: "Stop the operation."

The chief of staff edges forward, bracing his left arm on the compass, and salutes the admiral. A prolonged silence.

The admiral returns the salute, and the eyes of the two men meet.

The highest responsible officer of this incomparably ill-planned mission and his chief assistant.

Now the cruel defeat they had foreseen has finally become reality and is upon them.

All the words of admonition. All the frustrations. All the self-scorn. All the resentment.

A thousand conflicting emotions.

Still returning the salute, the admiral looks calmly to left and right and meets the glances of the surviving officers, one by one.

He shakes hands warmly with the several staff advisors who crawl up to him.

For a moment he seems to smile. That may be an illusion, for I have always dreamed that brave men smile in such situations.

Turning his tall body about, he departs via the ladder to the admiral's private quarters directly under the bridge.

Thus comes to an end the role the admiral has played in our presence, he who since the battle began has remained utterly aloof and has not stirred in the slightest.

Thereafter, until the ship sinks, the door to the admiral's private quarters does not open. Nor do we hear, perhaps because of the ceaseless sounds of destruction, the report of his pistol.

Fondling his pistol, did he experience with his own body the death of the ship?

Thus the last moments of Vice Admiral Itō Seiichi, commander in chief of Task Force II.

The task force herewith loses its leader. Soon it will lose its main citadel as well.

Seeing the admiral depart for his private quarters, his adjutant, Lieutenant Commander Ishida, nimbly follows in his steps.

Because it has been his job from beginning to end to wait on the admiral, he wishes also to share his death.

Instantly, with one bound, the chief of staff grabs him firmly from behind.

The adjutant, two or three rungs down the ladder, bent on hurrying down. The chief of staff, one powerful hand grasping the adjutant by the belt, the other gripping the railing, teeth clenched and entire face flushed.

Neither says a word, and for several seconds they are deadlocked.

"You don't have to go. Don't be a fool." Groaning in a low voice, the chief of staff. To withstand the full strength of the young adjutant must be an enormous strain.

The adjutant is surely the stronger of the two; but perhaps he loses heart in the face of the sincerity of the chief of staff. With face averted he finally yields.

With the same force with which he pulled him back up onto the bridge, the chief of staff now pushes him violently away.

Fortunately, both chief of staff and adjutant returned alive from the mission.

The two of them, I hear, having learned that things were not going well after the war for the admiral's bereaved family, which had lost both its men, contributed thereafter to its support insofar as each was able.

The Fateful Moment

I encounter Ensign Matsumoto at the rear of the bridge. His face pale, he points with his finger and whispers: "For us, too, it's only a matter of time, isn't it."

He is pointing toward the stern, at the aft weather deck, the topmost deck, highest above water level.

From the port, the side to which the ship lists, waves lap at the deck, and a run of waves washes it.

That aft weather deck, praised as a floating castle.

With waves striking the deck, it is already impossible to avoid capsizing.

Is he shuddering at this proof that our situation is hopeless? Gentle-hearted poet, Ensign Matsumoto. Has he already fallen victim to his own keen susceptibilities?

His post is on the second bridge several flights down, so he probably came up from there seeking companionship.

Did he expect me to be optimistic? He should be undaunted no matter how adverse the conditions; did he come seeking words of encouragement?

At this point I still do not dream that *Yamato*'s final gasp is near.

My mind has realized long since that the end is near; but my emotions, a different matter, blaze up, irrationally.

Is it because of the severe strain that has gone on so long? Or have I been bewitched by the magnificence of this giant ship?

All giant things have about them a mystique that captivates all those affiliated and instills in them an absolute trust and affection.

Those still alive on the bridge number no more than ten.

Some are in a great hurry to try and escape. They are all veteran officers: captains, commanders, and lieutenant commanders.

Crawling along the ladder, which is canted almost to water level, they turn their heads and cast furtive glances at us.

Where are they going, leaving their posts? Can there be a more appropriate place to die?

Let those who leave leave. But can it be that at this rare opportunity, this moment between life and death, they feel in their hearts not the slightest remorse?

Fortunately, at this point the rest of us are content with our lot. Something to be grateful for.

Around me it becomes quieter and quieter.

Though there is no letup in the sounds of destruction hastening the end of the fighting, I am oblivious; only a gentle silence touches my ears.

Everything I see shines with a white light. I gaze in wonder, as if my eyes were seeing things for the first time.

Have my eyes become crystal clear to their very depths?

Space comes to a stop before me; time freezes around me.

I am I and yet not I.

Barely a few instants, this interval.

Again, the voice from inside my chest presses me, virtually out loud.

"You, I pity you. Finally given in to death?

"You who are dying: what have you made of yourself?

"Think: do you have anything at all to be proud of?"

"Hold on, you! Wait! Please wait!

"My brief life *has* had its blessings—

"Warm ties to my parents. Wonderful teachers and friends. A pleasant environment. Rich hopes. Not inconsiderable talents—

"That's enough for me. I'm happy."

The voice: "Which of those represents the real you?

"Apart from all those, is there anything else that you, dying, would take with you? If there is, out with it!"

". . . no, those aren't the only things. There are others, glittering, unfading . . ."

The voice: "Tell me about them."

"Those many memories. Beautiful ones, free of all regret . . ."

The voice: "Are they true memories?"

"Ah, what is it, this uneasiness? Why this impatience?"

The voice: "Well, then, have you known the joys and sorrows that come from being modest? Have you bowed your head in true humility?"

"Ah, modesty? . . . I'm a proud one. Please forgive me. Still, allow me to reply that I acted once and once only in a way that, I believe, was almost modest."

The voice: "Was that true humility?

"Humility in the face of what? How did you show it?"

I cannot stand this self-questioning. Indignantly:

"Cut it out. Don't cross-examine me. I'll be the judge of myself."

The voice, with a derisive laugh:

"Judge yourself? Ha!

"You fool. Judging yourself even as you are being engulfed in the stench of death! Still deceiving yourself even at this late hour?"

"Leave me alone. Don't take this last brief moment of ease too from me. . . .

"I'm sinking: where am I going?

. . . .

"Please kill me. Rescue me from this fathomless terror.

"Kill me."

Last Dispositions

The captain: "How about the portrait of His Majesty?"

From the man in charge, Hattori, chief of the ninth division, comes a hastily written response delivered by messenger:

That he has the imperial portrait in his quarters and has locked the door from the inside. There is no surer way than this, to protect it with his life.

I see the navigation officer (a commander, responsible for the operation of the ship) and the assistant navigation officer (a lieutenant junior grade, his assistant) face each other and bind themselves together.

Knees rubbing and shoulders touching, they attempt to bind each other's legs and hips to the binnacle.

Not only would it be a matter for shame if by any chance they should float to the surface. But it is also a physiological fact that if they were thrown into the water with their arms and legs free, they would struggle to reach the surface; should that happen, the anguish would be too much for them to bear.

Seeing them, I too naturally reach for my side, touching the line readied some time ago. That such might be the end of a special attack was something we fully foresaw.

"What are you doing? You young ones, swim!" Chief of staff Morishita strikes a threatening pose, lacing his angry words with blows of his fists. He hits me from the side.

I have no choice but to follow his orders and, changing my mind, throw away the line; still, my resentment does not go away.

Grinding my teeth, I glare around me—if we try to get away now, what has been the purpose of this special attack mission? Why the line with which to end our lives?

The truth of the matter. Several minutes earlier, in that final conference to which the staff crawled its way, the commander in chief had given the order: "Stop the mission. Turn back after rescuing the men." Close to them though we were, we didn't know.

On the flag deck of *Yamato,* now little more than a skeletal structure, signal flags to that effect were hoisted immediately. The emergency beacon on *Yamato*'s main tower desperately signaled again and again to the destroyers on either side: "Move in closer! Move in closer!"

Yet the destroyers did not close us, fearing either the currents that would follow our sinking or the shock waves from the accompanying explosions. Had they come alongside, there can be no doubt they would have been dashed to pieces along with *Yamato.*

On seeing the signal to close us, the captain of *Fuyutsuki* is said to have flown into a towering rage. He refused to countenance the report of his senior officer that they were ready to come alongside to rescue the men and steamed off in the opposite direction.

He must have resented fiercely the fact that the change in plans was so cowardly: the sudden shift from the headlong rush of the special attack to miscarriage and flight homeward.

The staff officers who fled the bridge in great haste a moment ago had seen, shining toward them, a single ray of hope for survival.

Having heard with their own ears the decision to turn back, they acted so as to prolong their lives.

Had we too been privy to that order, what would we have done? Would we have been able to endure calmly the inner turmoil? Ours was the reckless valor of ignorance.

Those who take heart on seeing life beckoning turn weak; those who offer themselves up seeing no life beckoning turn strong.

Still, it was a resolute act, Admiral Itō's order to abandon the mission.

Of his comrades on the road to death, half were gone; for the desperate mission, there was no hope. The journey too was half over, and there was just enough fuel to get home if he turned back now.

The very last chance to act, a situation permitting no procrastination.

What extraordinary resolve! At the time, "One hundred million deaths rather than surrender" was a popular slogan; nevertheless, acting on his own initiative, he called a halt to this special attack mission on which so much had been staked.

One might say that in the end he carried out his original aim, for from first to last he had been stubbornly opposed to the mission.

Vice Admiral Itō, who at the time the war started was already in the important post of vice chief of the naval general staff. Since then he had been responsible for devising the strategy of all the important naval battles and had mourned the loss of countless vessels and men. It must have been his cherished ambition to die in the line of duty as commander of the last task force sent into battle by the Imperial Navy.

The commander in chief's sole concern undoubtedly lay in the consistency of his judgment on the merits of the mission's goal and of his execution of the plan. He staked everything on his firm adherence to this one point.

The horizon stands at right angles to the narrow lookout ports; chops my range of vision into two parts, black and white; presses in on me.

List: 80 degrees.

Over the voice tube, a message from a code officer: the code books have been attended to—he has taken all the classified documents in his arms, has entered the code room on the bridge, and has locked it from the inside.

The code books, so designed as to make it impossible for them to fall into enemy hands. Sheets of lead are attached to the covers of the books to make doubly sure the books sink; what is more, the codes are printed with a special ink that dissolves on contact with sea water; on top of that, a second strong impression is made with a matrix of different type to eliminate any physical imprint left by the type. And still the code officers must protect the top-secret codes with their lives.

The captain repeats the order: "All hands on deck." The captain's messenger transmits it orally to each division.

So few still alive!

It was clear that it was already too late; but measures

had been taken against sinking, and the captain hoped to save even a single life, and more if possible.

Ah, at that moment did even one sailor take this order to mean, "All hands, prepare to abandon ship"?

The desperate battle developed halfway to our destination on this most funereal special attack mission ever; at its close, did anyone have even the slightest expectation of surviving?

Furthermore, the men in *Yamato* had no way of knowing that the mission had already been canceled for the other ships, that it had been decided to rescue the men and head for home.

"All hands, prepare to die." Wasn't that the only order we expected to hear?

We knew intuitively that "on deck" meant to assemble on deck for a final standing at attention at quarters, prepared for death.

Even if the end of *Yamato* did not come within the next few hours, we had used up more than half our fuel, and there was not enough left to make it back. There was nothing for the survivors but to make a furious dash at the enemy.

In any case, the order to rescue the men came too late.

I saw several of the hatches scattered on the forward deck open from inside and men race up and out, but now the water covers the area like a smooth cloth and pours down the hatches.

Escape from the Bridge

The bridge is already just a dark chamber lying on its side.

Two volumes of operation documents, fallen from somewhere: without thinking, I pick them up and put them away in the chart stand.

Around me, all at once, I see no one.

The command "All hands on deck," manipulating the exhausted survivors like puppets, has lured them to leave the bridge.

My post: should I leave it? The bridge: a capital place to die.

Nothing left for me to do here?

These twenty square meters of space, to which I have entrusted my fate, to live or to die, for these two hours.

For a moment, an involuntary restlessness.

As if possessed by something, I stick my fingers in the grating of the deck and clamber up onto the lookout stand.

Some guy ahead of me kicks me, and I roll off onto the bottom of the bridge; but grumbling "Here I go again," I crawl up onto it once more.

Behind me, a cheerful voice: "Okay, I'm bringing up the rear." Ensign Watanabe, communications officer.

He was stationed on the bridge in place of the wounded Ensign Nishio; as a result he is lucky and survives. The last to escape from the bridge; he reports that when he had climbed halfway out the port he and the ship were engulfed together by the water.

He went through the window, he says, as if blown out by the pressure of air or water; he was thrown into the sea.

Wriggling through the port, I look back almost longingly: poor bridge, on its side and completely dark. Surprisingly narrow, burrowlike.

Their bodies lashed together, the navigation officer and the assistant navigation officer reject a second and third time our exhortations to escape; they shrug off their shoulders the hands of their fellow officers.

I watch until the end: both have their eyes wide open and stare fixedly at the water rising toward them.

Thus the end of Commander Mogi and Lieutenant (jg.) Hanada.

Is the responsibility of running the ship so great?

Even now vivid in my memory: the voice of Ensign Mori, an aide attached to the captain, continuing to shout encouragement; and the sight of him, thumping the sailors on the shoulders with a swagger stick, right up to the moment of sinking.

For him who never did take off his steel helmet and flak jacket, it is an admirable end.

Because we were posted on the enclosed part of the bridge, we had no such protective gear. To go into the water still wearing such gear makes it impossible to stay afloat for any length of time.

The Great Whale Sinks

I crawl out the lookout port and stand on the starboard bulkhead of the bridge. The survivors are lined up on the brownish belly of the ship, a distant thirty or forty meters away, all with hands raised in unison. They must just have finished three shouts of *banzai!*

In a small cluster and moving as one, they look like toy soldiers; my heart goes out to them.

The last moments of Rear Admiral Ariga Kōsaku, captain of *Yamato:*

In the antiaircraft command post on the very top of the bridge, still wearing his helmet and flak jacket, he binds himself to the binnacle.

Having completed the final dispositions—the codebooks, the command for all hands to come on deck, and so on—he shouts *banzai* three times. On finishing, he turns to look at the four surviving lookouts standing by his side.

They are too devoted to this resolute ruddy-faced captain to be able to leave him. Seeing a resolve to die together crystallizing among them, he slaps each on the shoulder, encourages them to keep their spirits up, and pushes them off into the water.

The final sailor presses his last four biscuits into the captain's hands, as if to show his innermost feelings. The captain takes them with a grin. As he has the second one in his mouth, he is engulfed along with the ship.

To eat biscuits at such a time! Iron nerves without equal.

Thus the words of the chief lookout. He too was unable to leave the captain's side. In the end he was thrown into the water while standing right next to the captain; but not having lashed himself down, he floated to the surface.

Fluttering atop the main mast, the great battle ensign is about to touch the water.

As I watch, a young sailor comes forward and clambers up to the base of the mast. Would he serve the battle ensign, soul of this sinking giant?

No one could have ordered him to do so.

So he has chosen this glorious duty. How proud his death!

It seems foolish to think such thoughts now, but when I drop my glance to the hull of the ship towering above the water and to its exposed undersides, it looks like a great whale.

That this vast piece of metal, 270 meters long and 40 meters wide, is about to plunge beneath the waves!

I recognize near me many shipmates. That fellow, and that one.

This one's eyebrows are very dark, that one's ears very pale. All of them have childlike expressions on their faces; better, they are all completely without expression.

For each of them, it must be a moment of absolute innocence, an instant of complete obliviousness.

For all I know, I too am in the same condition.

At what do they gaze with ecstatic eyes?

The eddies, extending as far as they can see. The boiling waves, interlocking in a vast pattern.

Pure white and transparent, like ice congealing around this giant ship and propping her up.

And the sound of the waves, deafening our ears, induces still deeper rapture.

We see a sheet of white; we hear only the thundering of the turbulent waters.

"Are we sinking?" For the first time, as if on fire, I ask myself that question. The spectacle is so mysterious, so resplendent, that I am overcome with the premonition that something extraordinary is about to happen.

The water already begins to creep up on the starboard half of the ship.

Bodies flying in all directions. It is not simply a matter of being swallowed by the waves. The pressure of the water boiling up sends bodies flying like projectiles.

The bodies become mere gray dots and scatter in all directions, effortlessly, happily. Even as I watch, a whirlpool runs fifty meters in one swoop.

And spray springs up at my feet; water contorted as in a fun-house mirror, gleaming in countless angles, countless formations, glitters before my nose.

In multiple mirrors the water engulfs human figures. Some pop back up; some hang upside down in the water.

This exquisite glass design colors the uniform white of the foam, as do stripes of pure blue scattered all over this blanket of bubbles. The effect of the churning created by the many eddies?

Just as my heart delights for a moment in this beauty, this gracefulness, I am swept into a large whirlpool.

Without thinking, I draw as deep a breath as I can.

Grabbing my feet and rolling up into a ball, like a baby in the womb, I brace myself and do my utmost to avoid being injured; but the snarling whirlpool is so strong it almost wrenches off my arms and legs.

Tossed up, thrown down, beaten, torn limb from limb, I think: o world, seen with half an eye at the last moment. Even twisted and upended, how alluring your form! how exquisite your colors!

This mental image, flitting past, is welcome solace for my suffocating breast.

Not one person managed to swim far enough away in time to escape this whirlpool.

They say that with a great ship like this one, the danger zone has a radius of 300 meters.

The decision to save the men came too late and robbed us of the margin of time needed to swim that distance.

All hands dead in battle—this has become our fate.

Explosion

Now *Yamato*'s list is virtually 90 degrees.

Such instances are rare. Most ships sink when the list reaches 30 degrees.

Because of the 90-degree list, the shells for the main batteries fall over in the magazines, slide in the direction of their pointed ends, knock their fuses on the overhead, and explode.

This reconstruction of events was agreed upon at a staff conference of the officers after our return. The staff officers recognized that at the time no fire could have reached the magazines.

The ship is already completely under water; I am in the whirlpool.

There is a full load of shells for the main batteries: armor-piercing shells, one round of which can sink a ship, and type-3 shells, one round of which can knock out a squadron of planes.

First, the fore magazine explodes. Twenty seconds after the ship went under?

Had it happened before the sinking, with the ship still on the surface, the explosion would have turned us outright into shrapnel and scattered us in all directions.

But the water, even while toying with us, deadened its force.

Had there been no explosion, I would have sunk rapidly in the whirlpool, to the bottom of the sea.

At the instant *Yamato,* rolling over, turns belly up and plunges beneath the waves, she emits one great flash of light and sends a gigantic pillar of flame high into the dark sky. Armor plate, equipment, turrets, guns—all the pieces of the ship go flying off.

Moreover, thick smoke, dark brown and bubbling up from the ocean depths, soon engulfs everything, covers everything.

The navigation officer on one of the destroyers calculated that the pillar of fire reached a height of 2,000 meters, that the mushroom-shaped cloud rose to a height of 6,000 meters.

Newspapers reported afterward that the flash of light could be seen easily from Kagoshima.

Opening out like an umbrella, the top of the pillar of light engulfs and destroys several American planes circling to observe the end.

In the general explosion, the shells for the main batteries, carried below decks but of no use because of the bad weather, do get their shot at the enemy.

The pressure generated by the explosion of the fore magazine alone is not equal to that of the whirlpool.

While being tossed about in the whirlpool, my whole body absorbs the extraordinary concussion of the shock wave from the first explosion; I am thrust back, around, and up, crashing into a thick yet undulating wall overhead.

This wall: the corpses of comrades who surfaced quickly and are now being baptized in the fiery rain.

Did they shield us with their bodies from the arrows of fire?

Meanwhile, the whirlpool still has enough force to pull us back down again, away from the surface.

Then, about twenty seconds later, the second explosion. Perhaps part of the aft magazine?

This blast finally hurls my body up to the surface.

The repeated explosions send countless pieces of shrapnel flying. Did the shrapnel turn all the men into living targets, save only those few of us on the aft side of the main tower?

Again, we alone were able to avoid fearsome injury from the underwater explosions.

To think that we who stayed put on the bridge and stuck close to the ship's superstructure should be protected time and again and be safest of all!

As for those who left before us and neared the deck, the nearer they were, the more exposed they were to the blasts.

What an irony!

Even so, every one among us is at least slightly wounded. Most have injuries to head and feet.

Only those whose wounds were slight were able to survive the hardships to follow.

I receive a long burn wound and a cut on the top left of my head. According to the examination carried out later by the medical officer, the fragment of shrapnel must have been pretty large, and chances were that the injury would have been a fatal one; but because it hit my head at a tangent, I narrowly escaped death.

It hit me while I was being tossed about as if by a hurricane. This being so, how tiny the probability that the piece of shrapnel and I should collide at a tangent!

To be born a human being and yet to owe my life to the fact that something hit me tangentially! Should I laugh?

A great number of men must have been sucked under by the funnel.

Fearsome, its suction. A great cavity sucks up a vast amount of water and, with it, any solid object.

After we got back the survivors were asked to mark on a diagram where they were when they entered the water. In the vicinity of the funnel: a large blank space.

Had I been five paces to the right, I would have been in danger.

The pillar of fire blows straight back down. The sky is filled with red-hot shrapnel and pieces of wood falling with a roar.

The debris kills or wounds most of the men who struggled to float to the surface but got there too soon.

Only those of us who float up at the last, after having taken the roundabout route through the whirlpool, escape that and do not see a scorching hot sky. Instead, we see only dense smoke.

Those who came to the surface a few moments earlier than we looked up as in a daze at countless pieces of metal falling out of a blazing orange sky.

Caught up in the whirlpool, my body suffered great torment. By comparison, how trivial the thoughts that flooded my mind!

. . . There was still a good bit of soda left in that bottle . . . and I've still got five packets of candy . . . late, isn't it? . . . from a quick look at the charts I know the ocean in this area is 430 meters deep; at this speed, how long before I sink to the bottom? what does it feel like to drop 430 meters? and, and then? . . .

Finally, still with only the one deep breath, I approach my limit.

Perhaps ten seconds after the shock from the second explosion, the agonizing pressure on my chest rises sharply; at last my throat seizes, and suddenly I start to swallow sea water.

Through my nose, through my mouth, I breathe in sea water as if poured in by a pump—unconsciously my body registers the movements of my jaw . . . seven . . . ten . . . fifteen . . . seventeen.

Still, I have no sense of suffocating. Am I unable to die until water fills all the nooks and crannies of my body and spills out my mouth?

Is the peace of death still far off?

Kill me . . . Death, take me.

The edges of my eyes register a dim light. The backs of my eyelids are yellowish. In my nostrils a burnt smell surges up. My feet feel light. Everything is hazy as in a dream, and my body floats in space. No sooner do I think these thoughts than I break through the surface of the water.

Had the second explosion come even five seconds later, my lungs would have burst. It would have been all over with me.

Only those survived who were delayed on a circuitous route just long enough to avoid the falling pillar of fire and yet were thrust to the surface before their lungs burst.

Lieutenant Watanabe: "The darkness turned bright, so I heaved a sigh of relief—'Hooray! It's the next world!' "

Cadet Sako: "I'm not sure, but I think I said two

prayers to Amida. Strange—I've never been one to pray."

To think that if even one element of this repeated good fortune had been lacking, we would not have seen the light of day again!

Cut off by the water, the smoke gradually clears away only to leave behind waves covered with bubbly heavy oil.

"*Yamato* sinks. 1423 hours." Friend and foe flash the message simultaneously.

Two hours of uninterrupted battle against airplanes. It's over now.

Adrift

The heavy oil smarts, and my eyes won't open. Catching my breath, I prise open my eyes, clean out my ears, and float for several minutes.

Gradually it registers that I am still among the living, not in the realm of the dead—damn! Have I floated to the surface? To live again?

A light rain falls upon the water as I do battle with heavy oil, cold, sweeping fire of machine guns, loss of blood, sharks.

Very close to me, waves shining the color of ash. The rough ocean swell viscous with heavy oil.

A layer of mucklike oil. A coating of bubbles. Drifting bits of wood.

Men singing to keep up their spirits. Voices sound, far and near, not in unison.

Men panting at the weight of their own bodies.

Men groaning with pain—probably the badly

wounded. Because the heavy oil turns everything a uniform black, we can't tell even red blood.

Some poor men go mad and sink. Swallowing oil has physiological effects. Their shouts sound like laughter, indeed, like the shrill voices of girls.

Those who thrash about too much disappear in the twinkling of an eye—the prey of hungry sharks attracted by their movements?

Many men use up their energy and drown. Many young sailors seem with their last breaths to call out their love for their mothers; then, with both hands raised as if trying in vain to grasp the sky, they go under and are gone.

A hoarse voice sounds across the water: "Anyone of warrant officer rank or better, stay where you are and report your names. Take charge of the men around you and stand by. Make preparations for staying afloat." The one doing the shouting, seen from the side—assistant gunnery officer Shimizu?

—Right, I am an officer, albeit not much of one. Take charge of the sailors. Gather together as many as possible. Wait for the next step.

Why have I been so absentminded? Will there ever be a better time to do my duty?—

Lifting my voice and waving my arm, I report my name.

Sailors whose faces are hard to tell apart slowly make their way through the waves and gather—I herd about ten into a group and make them wait quietly.

I try to do as we have rehearsed, using our leggings to tie a raft together to accommodate the wounded; but the explosion of the ship has blown all the wood into small pieces. None is long enough to make a raft.

Each of us must gather several bits of wood for himself, squeeze them under his arms or between his legs, and try for dear life to stay afloat. Holding them between our fingers doesn't work because our fingers quickly go numb.

I open my eyes, stinging from the heavy oil; I pursue something over the ocean swells as if possessed. What is it?

None other than an apparition of *Yamato,* that great hulk of metal, dark gray and towering into the sky.

All of us treading water pursue it with an insatiable tenacity.

Has it made me so fearful, so lonely, the disappearance of that which these feet of mine trod, that which supported my body?

Yamato—support of my life, now gone. Only bubbles, bubbles.

The strafing fire of machine guns. Planes that skim past, hugging the water, carefree.

Belts of bullet tracks that thread splashes into the face of the water. Paradoxically, a pretty sight when the belts intersect.

Terror? Not terror.

Why do the bullets steer clear of us?—Very strange.

The faces, the heads near me. Jet-black, monstrous. Like balls of charcoal the size of cantaloupes.

A smile bubbles up from within me—they are so comic—but I bite my lip and suppress the grin.

Then suddenly rage wells up within me. Spitting out the anger on the tip of my tongue and hissing, I glare around me.

124

I'm soaked all the way to my underwear.

Teeth chattering, I groan with the cold. I ball my fists and strike them together.

I am aware of only two things: my unreasoning anger, and the cold.

The piece of chair which I have been holding on to for dear life is forever submerging and causing me to swallow large amounts of water. I'm having too hard a time of it, and so I let it go. It sinks immediately.

Had sea water already soaked into all the straw of the cushion and increased its weight? Holding on to it was as stupid as holding on to a lead sinker.

"Good going!" I try to speak aloud and encourage myself, but my voice catches in my throat and all that happens is that my temples vibrate a bit.

When, of necessity, I turn to look for new pieces of wood, I meet the glance of a sailor nearby. He has eyes like a fish, timid and nervous.

"Don't worry, I won't steal your chance to survive. Why should I pick on you?" Muttering these words, I swim away from him.

Bobbing up and down in the water, I finally grab hold of several small pieces of wood.

With the pieces clamped under my arms, I look back; he is still twisting his body to face me, peering at me hatefully.

When I take a good steady look at him, I recognize the face: a radioman I know. A boy.

What could cause so great a change in the face of one so young?

Such resentment, such loathing; yet we are shipmates.

Are they so strong, the grudges and the distrust sailors feel toward officers? Even for a boy so naive?

Something presses up on my chest. To endure the pain I tense up my toes as I tread water.

To die of cold, I think, must be just like falling asleep, deep and easy.

So my present futile struggling must lead soon to that easy death.

All I need do is just wait like this for drowsiness to overtake me. So be it.

But what to do about the oil-smeared eyes, the panting mouths, the exasperated tenacity of the sailors gathered here in a flock?

It is only natural, of course, that they should struggle. Individual human beings engrossed in their own lives and in nothing else. Their true character is laid bare.

Coward that I am, I try to escape—into my own thoughts.

All I can hope is that when the time comes I die a good death. Intent, I spur myself on in this way.

Something occurs to me: apart from right now, will there ever come a precious moment when I can hear the music of the spheres?

I should be able to. If I am now absolutely receptive, I should be able to. Surely I can experience a single incomparable moment.

—Nothing. A silence like that of death.

In that case, haven't I some music of my own? My love of music, my conceit: was that all a lie?—Wait! What is it I heard just now, that just came alive in my breast?

Yes, of course, a theme of Bach. The theme from the

Unaccompanied Sonata, familiar to my ear, sustenance to my heart.

—Wrong. It's not real. A hallucination, isn't it?

No, don't let thoughts lead you astray. Don't think.

Just be your true self. As suits you, be afraid, lament, rejoice.

Had I known then that I had some chance of surviving, would I have been so tranquil?

Wouldn't I have fought, struggled for the slightest possibility of surviving, thrashed obstinately until my strength was spent?

Look: someone smiling in my direction. Leading Seaman Noro, with his boyish—indeed girlish—face.

He was never under my direct command. But several times on the bridge I used him to transmit messages.

A model sailor, he: intelligent, conscientious, outstanding.

Dark pieces of wood bob up and down in the water about his chubby cheeks. In his mouth, opening in a smile, the slight gleam of his teeth.

The expression on his face, appearing and disappearing in the waves, is without doubt a smile.

The affection. The bliss.

He is kind enough to delight in my escaping the whirlpool. He gives his blessing to the fact that we have set out together to swim the rough seas of this existence.

Eyes inflamed by oil, a smile selfless and innocent. Captivated, I smile in response.

I let up treading water, and in the next instant I get a faceful of wave.

Tears come to my eyes, tears overflow, and I turn away, ducking my nose into the oil.

How unseemly that the two of us together in the grasp of death should so revel in the rich bliss of life.

Still, to share a smile at such a time: what a feeling!

Are they tears of satisfaction, tears of relief that I have not yet lost a heart that can smile?

When the tears clear away, he is gone.

A destroyer advances toward us at full speed. Judging from its design, *Fuyutsuki?* We watch closely for a bit, and indeed the prow is headed precisely in our direction.

If she holds to this course, we will surely become fodder for her propellers.

Even while doubting that there is any point in getting out of its way, since we probably won't be rescued anyway, I lead the men slowly out of the destroyer's path.

At the moment of closest approach, she turns hard to one side, and the stern makes a wide swing to the left, plowing its way through the very middle of a group of floating men. It soaks them in its powerful wake and slides away.

We are in the middle of the downslope of the towering wake. With all of us holding on to one another, we fight the undertow.

Those who are several meters away from us, on the ship's side of the crest of the wake, are sucked into the demonic whirlpool created by the propellers. Drowned, every last one of them.

The destroyer signals repeatedly with five hand-held flags—has she put all her signalmen to work? "Hold on a bit." A bullet fells a signalman at his task, and another man immediately takes his place.

"Hold on a bit." Hold on for what?

Take heart—will they pick up those of us in the water,

use us to fill out the complement of the ships, and return to the attack?

The sailors who follow me are so immersed in their own lives that their eyes do not see, the flags do not register; jostling each other, they are engaged in singing military songs.

I put an end to that. Scolding them, I wait for what is to come.

Rescue

The destroyer makes one circuit of the men in the water and comes to a stop.

Although the enemy attack is over, planes are still to be seen. Stopping constitutes a real danger.

The ship can stop for only the briefest time. Will we be able to swim to her?

Measured by the eye, the distance from here is 200 meters.

Keeping the impatient ones in check, we advance in a group, pushing our pieces of wood. Must not rush things.

The alerts day and night, the two hours of fierce fighting, now the time in the water—our physical strength has already been pushed to the limit.

If we race, devoting all our remaining strength to the task, we will collapse when we get there; that much is clear. That is the lesson of past battles too numerous to mention.

The hems of our raingear, coiling around us; the weight of our high-top boots; the cumbersomeness of our leggings; the oil forming a thick layer on the surface of the water. Like thrashing around in honey.

Moreover, 200 meters to swim while husbanding our strength. If I can't get the men to follow me in this ticklish maneuver, what kind of officer am I?

The question crosses my mind: how much time has passed since we entered the water?

Barely twenty minutes? To go by how I feel, less than thirty minutes at the very most.

But in fact nearly three hours have passed since the ship blew up. Dusk is already settling on the ocean.

It would be natural for these abominable hours to seem longer than in fact they were; why is it that they seemed on the contrary much shorter?

Was it that staying afloat is completely mindless and fatiguing, that my sense of time is too fragile and I was simply oblivious of the minutes as they passed?

The sight of the rocking ship burns itself onto our eyes to the point of hurting; aching with intense desire, we arrive at last at the side of the ship.

We stop swimming, and my limbs are totally exhausted. All at once, perhaps because I have swallowed much oil, I feel feverish. Chills rack me.

Throw a line to desperate men and you see humanity stripped naked.

The oil becomes ever thicker. Heavy waves strike against the ship and bounce back. Chills and flashes of fever run up and down my spine.

Looking up in search of people, in search of voices, I am impatient beyond bearing.

O unfeeling ship! Would that your sides were vertical! But your hull is a wall towering over us, slanting outward pitilessly, almost covering us over.

Bitter despair fills me.

My eyes smart in the oil, and already I sense a paralysis in my lower limbs.

There are perhaps three lines hanging over the side; smeared with oil, they all glisten.

The many hands, too, covered with oil, glisten.

Individuals fighting among themselves to be first. Oil rubbing against oil.

Breaking off from my group and hurrying ahead, two sailors grab the lines, but the lines slip through their hands; sliding down, the two men disappear.

Was it their sense of relief, their feeling that "We're saved"? How absurd life is!

There is no chance that they will come to the surface again. That moment of heedlessness nullifies the long hours they have struggled to survive. How to overcome this obstacle? Here goes.

Grabbing the third sailor from behind and fastening my teeth on his right wrist, I use my teeth to strip off the oil. Got some skin too?—can't be helped.

I wind the line a couple of times around his wrist, binding it so tight that blood flows, and call up to the deck, "Hoist away!"

To the faces peering down from the deck, I signal by raising my hand. The line is pulled up slowly. One wrist barely supports the weight of one body.

Someone seizes hold of his ankle. "Lucky him, he's going to be saved!"—driven by that thought, and with that man's shoes dangling in front of his eyes, he grabs the foot with both hands.

Unlike lines, ankles are easy to hold on to.

One wrist is not strong enough to support the weight of two bodies. Together they lose their hold on the line and fall one atop the other—both gone.

That being the situation, I have to raise one person's wrist, pay heed to those directly beneath him, and beat back any arm that comes near.

The gleam of tenacity in the eyes looking up at the line!

The strength of their will to live: is it noble? is it base? Don't get led astray by your thoughts.

The sailors must be rescued, as many of them as possible. That is my duty.

Wishing to live, they are desperate. Wishing them to live, I too am desperate. This desperate struggle, impossible to avoid.

Am I right to exert such effort? wrong?

Has the power to determine who lives and who dies been given to me?

I don't know.

I just struggle, driven on by something involuntary.

Suddenly there are no more sailors.

How many have been saved? Only four?—the majority have sunk into the water and are gone. My fault.

A voice crying, "Hurry! Hurry!" Two faces peering down from the deck.

The ship slowly begins to move forward.

Unexpectedly, in front of my eyes, a rope ladder. It hangs down, twisting. The spot, very close to the stern, is already within the eddies created by the propeller.

It is my last, my very last chance. Pitching forward, I grab hold of the ladder. With the second joints of three fingers of each hand, I barely grab hold.

The waves beat relentlessly at the lower half of my body. I have no strength left to pull my body up.

My physical strength, which until this moment I have used extravagantly, even repeatedly striking several people, is gone on the instant as if it had all been a lie.

How wonderful the might of one who has risen above self!

For whatever raised me up like that, I am truly grateful.

But when I finally try to support myself, how feeble I am!

My strength falls away, seems about gone. It falters, as if to test whether I really am attached to life.

With half my body about to be carried away by the waves, I fight desperately against my own body.

—Let go? Shall I let go? Okay, just unclench my fingers a bit, let them slide off. That's all it takes.

To be at ease, a peace like that of sleep, death—I yearn to be at ease. I'll simply go ahead and die.

Ah, how sweet death is, how easy!

"You can do it! You can do it!" Voices of sailors from the deck above, piercing my ears.

They have witnessed my entire struggle. Shot through with real feeling, this encouragement.

A voice within me calls: "Live! Live! You've come this far; die and you're quits? Die and you needn't ask anyone's pardon?"

For the first time, for really the first time, the will to live fills me.

It is not a desire, that I should *like* to live; it is an obligation, that I *must* live.

Just as my physical body is on the point of dying, my soul finally ignites; with everything stripped away, only that which is truly me remains.

Within me, smeared as I am with blood and oil and entwined with the ladder, is this undying flame, and this alone.

This is the hour of my death, this hour of supreme bliss in which death is vouchsafed me.

For this very reason, this is also the hour in which I must make every effort to live.

Strong hands grab both my hands—it has been long, the hard struggle on the rope ladder.

Moment by moment, the choice: battling myself, to live? or giving in to myself, to die?

Two sailors wrest the ladder from my hands, throw me down on the deck. I lie as I fall, lacking even the strength to raise my head.

There is only the awareness, permeating my body in its utter exhaustion: no need any longer to support this body of mine with my own hands.

Ah, I must have been destined to live!

If by chance the sailors had been too hasty in pulling up the rope ladder, my fingers would have slipped right off the rung, and everything would have been over.

Taking into account my weight and my state of exhaustion, they do it just right. And this at a time when there is still danger of enemy attack: worthy crew members of a battle-seasoned destroyer.

The sailors quickly strip off my uniform, turn me face down, stick fingers down my throat, and make me vomit up the oil.

Their only question: "Do you have any valuables, sir?" Valuables—mission documents, secret materials relating to personnel, cash—it is a mission leading to certain death, so I carry none of these things. Valuables—no time for such things.

They spread a blanket over my naked body. It quickly becomes soaked with the oil that has penetrated to my skin and turns heavy, chilly. Shudders again run violently throughout my body.

"You've got a head wound, sir. To the sick bay, please." In response to this advice, I raise one hand to my head. The wound from that explosion is fully two fingers wide. Until now it hasn't hurt, so I haven't even noticed it.

Fortunately, the wound is to my head, and the bleeding stopped while I was swimming. If by any chance it had been to my neck or body, then for the long time I was in the water there would have been no way of stopping the bleeding. I would surely have died while swimming.

When I enter the passageway in search of the sick bay, corpses lie in heaps. There is no place to set my feet, and every few steps I stumble and fall.

What I fall onto is a floor of warm human flesh. How fitting that this ship should be *Fuyutsuki,* hardest fighting of them all!

Lying just as I have fallen in exhaustion, I see from one side the face of an officer who rushes past, shoving me out of the way as he goes.

Ensign Tanabe—dear school friend, university classmate. That's right—he did become navigation officer in *Fuyutsuki.*

I raise my voice and call to him. He looks me up and down, my whole body smeared with oil, and laughs aloud, "You really are a mess!"

135

I look at him hurrying past, and I see that he is crawling along the narrow passageway. He himself probably doesn't realize that he is on hands and knees.

It's already been twenty or thirty hours of ceaseless activity, with desperate tasks coming one on top of the other. His legs finally will support him no longer; there is no alternative but to crawl. Still, for him to laugh at how bad I look . . .

I get to the sick bay, and they stitch up my wound.

Two medical officers, bathed in the blood of others, wield their scalpels with a determined look.

They use the washroom as their emergency sick bay. So they can flush the blood down the drain.

If it were any other room, there would soon be a sea of blood. They would drown in blood.

In one corner of the room a great mound of corpses reaches up to the ceiling.

The patient before me in line is a young sailor whose ankle has been torn off. During the operation to amputate below the knee, there are of course no anesthetics. Perhaps because it hurts so badly, he cries like a baby.

When before his eyes the scalpel slices through the bone of his shin like a sharp knife through butter, his crying stops all of a sudden, and his body goes stiff. Had he lost too much blood?

The medical officers pick him up, one by the head, one by the legs, and after swinging the body energetically once, twice, heave it up to the top of the mountain of bodies.

My operation is easy; they open the wound, wipe away the oil, and sew it up expertly. They say there's almost no danger of infection.

They administer some eye medicine that stings. The irritation caused by the oil is acute.

To say that the ship smells of blood is an understatement. The deluge of blood reeks; I gag and have difficulty breathing.

At his battle station beside the binnacle, Lieutenant (jg.) Nakata, *Fuyutsuki*'s navigator, had bullets lodge in both forearms. Even though wounded, he carried out his duties until finally he fainted from loss of blood and was carried to the sick bay.

He receives emergency first aid and is ordered to rest; but seeing his chance he escapes and hurries toward the bridge. However, with both arms bandaged he cannot move freely; they find him halfway up the ladder, passed out again from loss of blood. A good man, twenty-one, with a fine mustache.

I hear for the first time of the decision to abandon the mission—that we have been picked up not in preparation for attacking, but in preparation for returning home.

That our present course is not south-southwest, but east-northeast. Speechless, I chew my lip.

Two hours after *Yamato* sank came the belated order from the headquarters of the Combined Fleet: "Call off the attack; pick up survivors and head for Sasebo."

It is good that the chief of staff did not go back on his pledge to take emergency action to bring the operation to an end; but by the time all the ships had completed their rescue operations, the evening mist had settled over the ocean battleground. That was inevitable.

With the end of the special attack mission in my ears,

I take no joy in having come back from the very brink of death.

Death is still close by. It is life, not death, which involves pain. And the conquest of self.

The pain from exhaustion and swallowed oil is severe, and I run a fever. The chills don't stop.

I go to the officers' quarters, collapse onto a bunk, and fall asleep—one of a pile of sleepers.

"Now hear this, crew of *Yamato!* All able-bodied men, assist in the operation of this vessel." Barking at us, Lieutenant (jg.) Yamamori. *Yamato*'s hot-blooded assistant navigation officer.

I crawl to the bulkhead and with difficulty pull myself erect. My face is a study in chagrin and frustration.

"Aye, aye!" respond voices nearby, but that is all; I see no one actually moving.

I know full well that those who have been rescued should help out, but my arms and legs refuse to do my bidding.

While in the water, one sailor saw Ensign Mori, aide to the captain. So Mori escaped the murky depths at the sinking, but still did not make it?

He who longed with his whole heart to die, who prayed that his fiancée would find a new life; he followed the road to death, unerringly, to its end.

He was an expert swimmer, but perhaps his uniform was too heavy or his wounds too severe.

Did he die in the line of duty, utterly intent, in his warmhearted way, on rescuing the sailors at the side of the ship, encouraging them, scolding them?

How did he challenge death, fight with death, finally attain death?

In so doing, did he bring his life to completion, ennoble himself?

For the vanquished, it is a difficult road that leads from here to Sasebo.

The crack American submarines, eager to feast on wounded destroyers, wait for us at several points; all night long they attack us persistently from the rear.

As if in a nightmare, I hear the buzzer incessantly calling the men to their stations, the submarine alert resounding through the ship.

It is said that when the crewmen of this ship walk through the passageways, the wounded men lying there reach up from the floor, grab their legs, and plead: "Please get us back safely to Japan!"

Moreover, damage to the instruments on the bridge is extensive, and casualties among officers and men are heavy. It is no easy matter to run the ship. But with indomitable fighting spirit and a deep sense of responsibility, and with these alone, they carry on the hard fight.

A last resort when one is encircled by enemy submarines is to shine searchlights on the nearest sub, fire ranging shots that force it to submerge, and then flee through the gap—I understand we performed that desperate maneuver repeatedly.

"Four torpedo tracks to starboard!"—voices reporting such messages pierce my ears as I lie in torment. Almost delirious, I mutter: "Okay, this time I'm not going to swim. Look. I'll really die."

This is how things go right up till dawn.

Yukikaze did take two torpedoes; but fortunately neither exploded, so she escaped harm.

The Remnants of the Task Force

Of the ten ships of the special task force for the thrust against Okinawa, only four ships are still functioning: *Fuyutsuki, Suzutsuki, Yukikaze,* and *Hatsushimo.* More than half the task force is gone.

Kasumi and *Isokaze* both took damage to their engines and are dead in the water. If left that way, they will be captured by the Americans and it will be impossible to prevent a breach of security.

There is no alternative but to sink them with our own torpedoes.

Entrusted with the task, *Fuyutsuki* heads for *Kasumi.*

The time for lying alongside is five minutes, and during that time a great stream of officers and men files across the two gangplanks fixed between the ships.

The officers all throw away their battle caps and wear their uniform caps. With official documents in hand and swords at their side, they salute the ship they are abandoning and come on board.

The junior officers and men stand in formation and wait their turn, or they hurry across carrying the wounded piggyback.

When five minutes are up, the gangplanks are knocked away simultaneously, even as men are still to be seen on board *Kasumi.*

We immediately pull away, and after the courtesy to the ship of one leisurely circuit around her, we finish her off expertly with a single torpedo, precisely placed.

After the enemy task force withdrew, *Yukikaze* headed for *Isokaze* and carried out the same procedure.

As for *Suzutsuki,* her commissioned officers and warrant officers have all been killed or wounded, and a senior petty officer has taken command. Moreover, her engines and boiler are damaged. She cannot move forward.

She signals *Fuyutsuki* by blinker, "Heading toward Kagoshima in reverse."

Later, having succeeded with desperate emergency repairs, she makes instead for Sasebo, farther away.

Fuyutsuki is in the best condition; 8 April, morning, we make port at Sasebo.

Yukikaze and *Hatsushimo* make port slightly later, at noon of the same day.

Suzutsuki enters the harbor still later, about dusk, stern aflame and on the point of sinking; she enters the drydock in that condition.

Tales Told by Some of Those Rescued

Executive officer Nomura of *Yamato* was rescued by *Yukikaze*'s boat. He is past his prime but still lean.

He is the sole survivor from the damage control station far below deck. How was he able to escape?

On a special attack mission the captain's death in battle is inevitable. The extremely important reports on the battle, the winding up of the affairs of the ship, and all such responsibilities fall to the executive officer.

No matter how difficult the situation, he must return alive.

When at last he reached the rescue boat, he was exhausted, indeed, about to go under; but seeing the captain's insignia on his uniform, the rescue crew quickly pulled him out.

They say that he was already utterly done in, that he was completely unconscious, and that they struck him repeatedly to keep him alive as they hurried back to the ship.

He has a long bullet wound from his forehead to the back of his head.

Ensign Kamata, the officer in charge of the machine guns at the very stern of *Yamato,* fights bravely until nearly the end of the battle; but when his guns take a bomb hit and stop functioning, he gathers all the men of his squad at the base of the turret.

He distributes some candy and hands around a cigarette, gift of the emperor, for each man to take a puff. Aware somehow that there is something still to be done, he becomes conscious of his need to urinate.

Ascertaining that his men all have the same thing on their minds, he laughs loudly, lines them up at the railing, and together they urinate into the ocean. Then he has them stand shoulder to shoulder and sends them flying into the water.

He himself, intent upon seeing all his men off for the final time, is two or three paces behind them. Perhaps for this reason, he alone is flung up rather than down by the propeller, which is revolving at slow speed.

Six meters in diameter, the propeller pulls all the sailors under in an instant, but then with its upward thrust it picks him up and sends him flying out of its whirlpool.

"A fearsome enormous thing pressed right in before my eyes and the next instant I fainted." That is his recollection.

He received a cut extending from his right shoulder to the left side of his belly; but his clothes were thick and

142

the wound fortunately shallow. He got away with only a slight infection.

The coxswain of *Hatsushimo*'s rescue boat says with a sigh: "There was one guy who clung to the side of the boat and just would not let go, so we had no choice but to pull him up; he wasn't conscious of what he was doing, and we had to really work on him." The man in question was Lieutenant Emoto, chief of the fire control division of *Yamato*.

On reaching *Hatsushimo*, Lieutenant Emoto was carried to the sick bay, apparently dead. After two hours of artificial respiration he finally revived. But they say his agony was unbearable to see. He had an injury received in the water and compression of the chest, both from the force of *Yamato*'s explosion.

He had already been left adrift and had survived several times. Six months earlier, while he was serving in the South Pacific theater as a senior officer of a destroyer, his ship had come under heavy bombing and had sunk; but he transferred the majority of his crew to a raft that stood ready on deck, drifted, and awaited rescue by a friendly ship.

Happening to encounter one of our coast defense ships in full flight, he had her come alongside while he transferred to her his entire crew. Immediately sending his men to battle stations, he himself went up to the bridge and, ignoring the captain, took over command of the ship and her guns. With great spirit and skill he got the ship out of danger and back to port.

By nature forceful, quick, and enthusiastic, he goes straight to the heart of things.

A gunnery officer picked up by *Hatsushimo*'s rescue boat divulges the following tale:

The rescue boat soon has a full load of sailors plucked from the water, and as they keep adding to the load, the situation becomes dangerous. If she picks up still more men, she can't avoid capsizing, with everyone going to the bottom.

Nevertheless, more and more hands cling to the side of the boat. Their grip is strong, and the boat's list reaches the point that something must be done.

At this juncture the boat's coxswain and petty officers draw the swords they have ready and free the boat by cutting the competing arms off at the wrist or by kicking the men away. It is a last resort, taken in the hope of saving those already in the boat. Still, for the rest of their lives they will see the faces, the eyes of those, who, hands chopped off, give up all resistance, throw back their heads, and sink out of sight.

And those who wield the swords, too, hurry around the boat, faces pale, soaked with sweat, panting. A scene of living hell.

One extraordinary happening is attested to by many survivors as with one voice. During the period the destroyer was dead in the water to rescue survivors, a single American reconnaissance seaplane intentionally circled over our heads. Those in the water were not sure; but many of the crew of the destroyer remember an uncanny silence as the plane circled at an extremely low altitude.

The ability to dash about in any direction is the very life of a destroyer; as soon as she comes to a complete stop she is extremely vulnerable. It would have been like shooting fish in a barrel to attack the destroyer from low in the sky; but the enigmatic circling of the reconnaissance plane acted as an absolute protective wall, sheltering us from being stormed by the fighter planes and bombers waiting at higher altitudes.

The hostility of the American forces to *Yamato* has always been intense. In this operation, too, their aim of annihilating us completely was clear from their torpedo attacks, their strafing with machine guns, and their follow-up attacks on the men in the water. Therefore, it is hard to conceive that the protective action of this reconnaissance plane was based either on orders from the command plane or on humanitarian considerations.

With the immense sky and ocean as our stage, we and the crew of the American plane were fellow warriors who had used every trick of the trade in carrying out our duties. Launching a fatal attack against a rescue ship in her extreme vulnerability must have been something their instincts as warriors would not permit. They were elite warriors, the chosen. It was beneath them to defile the final scene of the war between Japan and America.

Their true motive is apparent in the fact that as soon as the work of rescuing survivors came to an end, they immediately moved to chase and attack us with great tenacity.

Safe Return

8 April, morning.

Having slept one night, I have entirely recovered my strength. The temperature and sick feeling have gone away. But my eyes give me terrible pain; I cannot open them easily.

Going out on deck, I wash my face. The jet black of my skin has not faded in the slightest.

We even laugh at one another's grotesque appearance.

The ship is already running along the west coast of Kyūshū. Sunlight pours into my eyes. The hills of home are sparklingly beautiful.

An involuntary sigh: "All the same, it's good to be alive."

Still, these bright colors of spring, set against the deaths of countless comrades in arms, make me ashamed that I am still alive.

I comfort myself with the thought that returning alive was not our idea, that it was the result of luck. But one nagging question will not go away. Was it right that we should have been saved?

We enter Sasebo harbor.

As we drop anchor, an air attack is in progress against some of the factories of the naval port. Expressionless, we watch the black smoke.

"All *Yamato* crew, assemble." It has been a long time since we last heard that order.

Some of us wear tattered uniforms, some are wrapped in blankets, and some are half-naked. A procession of ghosts and goblins.

Assistant gunnery officer Shimizu glares around at us and speaks: "You look at ease, insolent, as if you'd just accomplished a pretty tough piece of work. Why should that be? That battle wasn't such a big deal.

"From now on you veterans will be all the more in demand. Soon, perhaps even this very moment, you will follow me to the attack. Okay?"

The gazes pouring in on him, the gloomy silence. The fatigue from our trip to death's door is too great.

That same night we enter a branch hospital outside Sasebo Naval Base.

Located on an isolated island to prevent breaches of security, it is a facility for the treatment of injuries.

Bodies clothed in white. A ward reverberating the whole night through with the sound of waves.

In the night air fragrant with flowers, we have much to think about.

Spring at its height and a long, leisurely convalescence are too tame, somehow, for us to accept. The slightly wounded all petition the commanding officer of the hospital, and we are permitted to leave the hospital even though our treatment is not yet completed.

We proceed to Kure and find innumerable letters from home awaiting us. But almost all the addressees are dead.

Sorting the letters and returning them to the senders: a heartrending task.

At the Kure personnel department we ask about new assignments.

The executive officer: "Luckily or unluckily, we survived. We will find better places to die. Anyone have anything to add?"

As if wishing to quell pangs of conscience for having survived, we petition blindly for special attack duty.

Our requests are granted, and we are posted again to special attack units.

Granted survivor's leave, I set off for an unexpected trip home.

On the way, I send a telegram.

My last testament has already arrived, so father and mother may have become reconciled to my death—please get ready to be happy.

I arrive home. Father, with no outward show of emotion: "Here, I'll pour you a drink."

Mother, with quiet excitement, works diligently on a feast into which she pours her love. My telegram, seen by chance in the letter rack—so soaked with tears that the letters have lost their shape.

Did I truly know that she would be so beside herself with grief at my death? Did I know how absolutely selfless she was?

That being the case, did I know how precious life is? how despicable the slightest pride in having seen actual combat?

Some Reflections

My experience of those few days: call it a special attack sortie? These slender reflections: a harvest gained by venturing into the realm of death and returning alive?

No. Not one of us in ten thousand expected to return alive.

I did not choose death of my own free will; rather, death seized me. There is no easier death.

It is not a death of the spirit; it is a death of the flesh. It is not the death of a human being; it is the death of an animal.

Indeed, it is not death but only a small taste of death.

Did I look death in the face for even a single moment?

After we sailed, did I ever scrutinize myself closely, as one should on the brink of death?

In the last moments, did I have even the slightest sense that life was worth living?

I do not know death. I have not come into contact with death.

What spared me a confrontation with death, I see now, was the extraordinariness of battle. And my sorrow for those who were dying, and the clearly adverse fortunes of the homeland.

Consider by way of contrast the deaths of those on the home front, the deaths of the countless victims of the war.

What would have happened if I on the bridge had had fathers and mothers living nearby, as they did? If brothers and sisters, what then?

What would have happened if I had had opportunity to escape, room for choice, independence, responsibility?

What if I had been living a life of misery? What if I had been merely a worthless sacrifice?

Death in a special attack is far easier.

No one put in my position would have acted any differently. That would hold true for all: old people, infants, children, women.

The road to an inevitable death is broad and smooth. Death itself is a commonplace, a matter of course.

We ought to revere death solely because it is natural. Just as we revere Nature.

If so, ask about our experience not on the grounds that we faced certain death.

Ask rather: How did we discharge our duties? Did we act unerringly?

Did I really do my part? Did I look death in the face in the line of duty?

No. Didn't I submit to death quite willingly? Didn't I cloak myself in the proud name of special attack and find rapture in the hollow of death's hand?

Yes.

That and no other was the reason for my cold and callow behavior.

Was I diligent in my everyday duties? Did I act with utmost sincerity in my every action? Did I do my best at every moment?

On all these points I was negligent.

And yet, callow and negligent though I was, this testing was conferred upon me. For what reason?

Should I be grateful for my good fortune in once having death bestowed on me?

Or should I be grateful for my good luck in having death snatched away from me?

Had I turned back at that moment, in that instant of confused struggle at the twilight crossroads, what then? What awaited me—death?

So dark, painful, destitute: death beyond doubt? No matter.

That which set me apart from so many shipmates and bathed me once more in the light of day: what was it?

An end to thinking!

Death has nothing to do with me.

When it was close to me, death paradoxically receded; only when one has lived out one's life in peace and tranquillity can one come face to face with death.

Living a constant and sincere life—there is no other path to a direct confrontation with death.

Make of yourself an empty vessel.

Make of this moment a turning point toward a life of constancy and dedication.

In the end, this operation was not a success. We lost more than half the task force and turned back when we were only halfway there.

From the commander in chief of the Combined Fleet came words of appreciation: "Thanks to the sacrificial bravery of this task force, our special attack planes had great success."

The air assault *Kikusui I* of 6–7 April, in concert with Operation *Ten'ichigo,* was a major action involving the launching of a total of 700 planes, most of which were involved in *kamikaze* operations. However, the American forces knew ahead of time that our surface forces would have no air cover; hence they could keep their powerful squadrons of fighter planes near Okinawa. Moreover, our forces did not achieve close coordination of land and sea operations. Thanks to their success and our failure, our losses amounted to more than 350 planes shot down or damaged. On the other side, of the losses reported by the American forces, I understand that most of the thirty ships damaged were damaged only slightly and that only three destroyers were sunk.

After the whole operation was over, the chief of staff of the Combined Fleet sent this message to the entire navy: "In the early part of April 1945 our naval special attack forces carried out a resolute attack, unparalleled in its ferocity, against enemy forces in the vicinity of Okinawa. This action greatly enhanced the traditions of the Imperial Navy and the glory of our surface units. Many brave men, the commander in chief of the task force in the fore, laid down their lives in the noble cause of defending the Empire. Their utter sincerity in serving the country goes straight to our hearts, and their unswerving loyalty will shine through the ages. I hereby acknowledge their meritorious deeds and notify the entire navy."

Yamato sank and her giant body lies shattered 200 miles northwest of Tokunoshima. 430 meters down.

Three thousand corpses, still entombed today.

What were their thoughts as they died?

The **Naval Institute Press** is the book-publishing arm of the U.S. Naval Institute, a private, nonprofit, membership society for sea service professionals and others who share an interest in naval and maritime affairs. Established in 1873 at the U.S. Naval Academy in Annapolis, Maryland, where its offices remain today, the Naval Institute has members worldwide.

Members of the Naval Institute support the education programs of the society and receive the influential monthly magazine *Proceedings* and discounts on fine nautical prints and on ship and aircraft photos. They also have access to the transcripts of the Institute's Oral History Program and get discounted admission to any of the Institute-sponsored seminars offered around the country.

The Naval Institute also publishes *Naval History* magazine. This colorful bimonthly is filled with entertaining and thought-provoking articles, first-person reminiscences, and dramatic art and photography. Members receive a discount on *Naval History* subscriptions.

The Naval Institute's book-publishing program, begun in 1898 with basic guides to naval practices, has broadened its scope in recent years to include books of more general interest. Now the Naval Institute Press publishes about hundred titles each year, ranging from how-to books on boating and navigation to battle histories, biographies, ship and aircraft guides, and novels. Institute members receive discounts of 20 to 50 percent on the Press's nearly six hundred books in print.

Full-time students are eligible for special half-price membership rates. Life memberships are also available.

For a free catalog describing Naval Institute Press books currently available, and for further information about subscribing to *Naval History* magazine or about joining the U.S. Naval Institute, please write to:

Membership Department
U.S. Naval Institute
291 Wood Road
Annapolis, MD 21402-5035
Telephone: (800) 233-8764
Fax: (410) 269-7940
Web address: www.usni.org